THE ECONOMICS OF CO-DETERMINATION

THE ECONOMICS OF CO-DETERMINATION

edited by

DAVID F. HEATHFIELD

First published 1977 by
THE MACMILLAN PRESS LTD
London and Basingstoke
Associated companies in New York
Dublin Melbourne Johannesburg and Delhi

ISBN 0 333 21198 7

Printed in Great Britain by
BILLING AND SONS LTD
Guildford, Worcester and London

Contents

Acknowledgements

The editor and publishers wish to thank Professor Benjamin Ward and the American Economic Association for permission to use 'The Firm in Illyria' from *The American Economic Review*, 1958.

A great debt is owed to the Anglo-German Foundation for the Study of Industrial Society and its Secretary General, Mr Peter McGregor, whose financial support for these seminars has made the process of cross-fertilisation and germination possible.

Dr E. J. Feuchtwanger not only organised the Southampton end of the exchange but also translated, with assistance from Miss M. Holden and with financial support from the Anglo-German Foundation, the papers by Almanasreh, Abb and Kosta; Professor Gäbler was his own translator. The index was compiled by Alan Ingham.

Editor's Preface

In September 1975 the Anglo-German Foundation for the Study of Industrial Society sponsored the eighth annual joint seminar of the Universities of Frankfurt and Southampton. The theme of the seminar was 'Participation', and economists from both universities exchanged papers on Industrial Democracy.

Industrial Democracy has been discussed by politicians, social reformers, trade unionists and industrialists; but until comparatively recently has attracted very little attention from economic theorists. (A notable exception would be Cole [1972] [1973]). The 'theory of the firm' is still largely rooted in the idea of a profit-maximising entrepreneur, and this idea has been weakened only slightly by the recognition of the fact that power has passed from the owners of capital to their hired managers. The further movement of power, from managers to workers, lends descriptive, as well as prescriptive, force to those theories of the firm which admit the objectives of workers as maximands. This shifting of power is recognised politically in that 'national economic debates' involve Government, trade unionists and management – but shareholders are rarely mentioned. This could of course be a recognition of the legal requirement that management must act in the interests of the shareholders. On the other hand it is not very clear how managers can know what is in the interests of their now very diverse shareholders. Nor is it clear how shareholders can censure or even judge the performance of their managers. These problems of how to motivate and control managers can only partly be resolved by giving managers shares in the equity of their enterprise.

Traditionally, the influence of workers on management has been through trade unions which saw their role as much wider than simply maximising the incomes of those currently employed in a particular firm. Trade unions had, and continue to have, social, political and educational aims, organised on a national rather than a plant level. This perhaps has imbued the trade union movement in the United Kingdom with a sense of social responsibility which has restrained its use of its growing industrial power. Nevertheless the fact of this power has to be recognised, and at least some support for worker participation in the management of industry has come from those who wish to put responsibility where the power is. Others seem to think that participation will moderate the 'exploitation' of workers by capitalists and thereby redistribute income and wealth in favour of labour. Yet others believe that workers benefit from participation *per se*; workers are somehow made better, more complete individuals by having some direct influence on the decisions taken at their places of work. Still others argue that the principal gains are that workers will be better motivated and better informed by being involved in the firm's decision making. Each of these claims (and others) is examined in this volume.

The stage is set, as it were, by reprinting Ward's seminal article (Ward [1958]). Ward uses a partial-equilibrium, short-run framework, to compare the standard profit maximising entrepreneur's results, with those for a workers' co-operative. In such a co-operative, land and capital are hired at fixed rates from the government, and workers decide on output, employment, and product price. For perfectly competitive markets Ward concludes:

1. A change in the fixed costs to a co-operative results in a change in output in the same direction, whereas for an entrepreneur output is unaffected by fixed costs.
2. A change in the price of the co-operative's product leads to a change in output in the opposite direction. For the entrepreneur the changes would be in the same direction. The co-operative result is weakened if there is more than one variable input.
3. For imperfect competition an increase in demand leads to a decrease in co-operatives' output if they are operating beyond the maximum average product but leads to an increase if average product is still increasing. The fixed costs results of I hold under imperfect competition.

These results have been extended by Meade [1972] [1974] and Domar [1966], Vanek [1970] and Drèze [1975]; but the essential point established in this kind of analysis is that the change in control results in a change in behaviour and outcome.

In the paper which follows, Pearce shows that, in a general equilibrium context, the outcome is not changed, and is quite independent of the nature of the controlling factor. The difference between Ward and Pearce must clearly turn on the behaviour of those variables regarded by Ward as fixed. Pearce does not specify microeconomic or macroeconomic adjustment mechanisms–there is, for example, no government reaction function ensuring that full employment will be maintained. Rather, it is simply assumed that some minimum conditions for a social optimum are to be met, whatever the form of industrial organisation. These conditions are:

(i) Production is efficient
(ii) All markets are cleared
(iii) All factors are fully employed

(iv) Like factors receive like rewards
(v) Minimum costs
(vi) No restrictive practices

If these, undisputably worthy, conditions are brought about by government planning, chance or whatever, then all systems of organisation will give rise to the same set of outputs and prices. This is so in perfect or imperfect competition, with or without constant returns to scale. It can be abrogated only by abandoning money and prices in favour of central control over 'the minutest details of economic life'. This is interesting, not only as a well-defined defence of the rightness and immutability of a 'natural' outcome; it also, by denying claims that income will be redistributed by worker participation, indicates where one may look for such changes. Pearce, then, not only restates a belief in *laissez-faire*, he also indicates how some of the perceived 'injustices' which have been attributed to entrepreneurical capitalism may have arisen from unequal opportunity or inherited wealth for which worker participation is not an appropriate remedy.

Hawkins provides a critique of the Pearce approach. he argues that production is as much a sociological process as it is a physical one, and hence systems of industrial organisation, actually change the production function. X-efficiency will improve if workers believe that they are working for themselves or for society in general, rather than for some privileged group of capitalists. It is clearly difficult to quantify, or prove, the existence of any such effect. The introduction of the sociological element also destroys the possibility of inter-firm or international comparisons, since the different groups have different tastes, expectations and abilities. Participation may improve the productive performance of Swedish car workers, but may detract from that of their British counterparts. This being so, the examination of participation is an empirical rather than a theoretical matter.

Hawkins also raises the question of what the objectives of worker representatives would be: may they not be the same as those of the managers of today; and is there any evidence that workers have more information, or better managerial aptitude, than those chosen as managers under the existing system? On the other hand, if worker participation does reduce the disruption caused at the workplace in pursuit of sectional interests, then productivity would be improved in both the short and the long run. In fact neither Hawkins nor Pearce examines how a conflict of interest may be resolved under worker participation, as compared, for example, with the current system of negotiation and 'industrial action'. If participation is a cheaper way of reaching agreement would not entrepreneurs now use it?

There is also the question of how the central authority can maintain the full employment assumed by Pearce and questioned by Hawkins.

The problem is: can macroeconomic control be better exercised under a system of worker participation or under the entrepreneurial capitalist system? These and other questions are taken up by Gäbler, whose paper is tentative and exploratory – seeking to raise questions rather than provide answers. He sees participation in the context of West German experience, in which both workers and owners have representatives on a Works Council. With this shared control, the Works Council will express some combination of owners' and workers' objectives. The questions raised by Gäbler are then to do with (a) how the aims of workers will be changed under this mixed system; (b) whether there will be an unholy alliance between capitalists and workers within each industry, at the expense of consumers on the one hand and potential workers on the other; and (c) to what extent will macroeconomic control be altered by this form of participation.

The same kind of question is raised by Kosta in the context of the New Economic System in Czechoslovakia. The New Economic System required social ownership of the means of production, national economic planning, the use of some markets and democracy of decision-making. This accords much better with the Ward model than does the West German experience and hence provides a better proving ground for his results. Democracy of decision-making was introduced by the Czechoslovaks as 'a compromise between the principles of self-management and expert-management'. It was aimed at resolving, or at least easing, two problems: first, the conflicts between the few central planners and the numerous plant managers; and, second, the conflicts within each enterprise. But worker control was viewed not only as a means of resolving conflicts in an economically efficient manner – it was also regarded as an end in itself. Kosta's paper is particularly valuable in that it is an account of an actual social experiment allowing participation of workers in economic decision-making. The experiment was unfortunately interrupted by the replacement of the Dubček regime, but nevertheless Kosta's account provides invaluable insights into the problems experienced at both plant and national levels.

In the United Kingdom there is very little experience to draw on; and if anything our trade unions seem to have been less attracted to the idea of participation than their German opposite numbers. This may be due to the differences in outlook between the two – the British trade unions (classified by trade) regard production decisions as, at most, peripheral to their main functions, whereas workshop organisation is a central issue for the German trade unions, which are classified by industry.

One effect of the United Kingdom's membership of the European Economic Community, with its common industrial legislation, has been the renewed discussion of participation. Trades Union Congress (1974) outlines the view taken by Congress of industrial democracy, and does so firmly in terms of collective bargaining. Worker participation seems to be seen as being organised by and through established trade union hierarchies.

There is now a growing recognition that, at least in industries under public ownership, provision should be made at each level in the management structure for *trade union representatives of the workpeople* employed in those industries, to participate in the formulation of policy and in the day-to-day operation of their industries (p. 21, my italics).

This trade union involvement in the nomination of worker representatives on works councils applies in most European countries (France, Belgium, Denmark, Italy and the Netherlands), but in West Germany any employee may be nominated by any 10 per cent of the labour force.

Even with this heavy trade union involvement in worker participation there are few cases where workers have any real power over the decision-making bodies of Western European firms. It is very rarely possible for workers' representatives to form a majority on policy-making committees. Thus Western European experience of worker participation is largely in terms of an extension of the communications between labour unions and management, rather than a change in the controlling factor.

West German experience is outlined in Almanasreh's paper. It begins with some historical (post-1945) reasons for the West German trade unions forming local plant organisations within the context of entrepreneurial capitalism rather than going for co-determination and socialism. Working within the externally-imposed political framework, unions have sought greater participation and more equal income and wealth distribution; but the impression is that principles give way to pragmatism and short-run objectives begin to dominate.

The paper also deals with collective bargaining rights of trade unions under the Labour Constitution Act and the Co-determination Act for the German coal and steel industries; and also refers to plans to improve the system of participation in other industries.

Co-determination forms but one of the concerns of German trade unions, and Abb's paper describes how the emphasis has been shifted from one policy to another since 1945. Social Security has remained a central issue since 1945 but early efforts at encouraging co-determination gave way to more direct attempts to alter the distribution of property; these in turn gave way to wages policy. To date wages policy and changes in the social security system have been far more successful than participation in attempts to make the distribution of property more equal. This lack of success of participation may be due, in part, to the minority position of workers' representatives. If there were equal voting power (or even a majority of worker votes), then minor improvements in income and wealth distributions might be achieved, but probably at the cost of forgoing some freedom of action of workers in disputes.

The advantages to the workers in particular, or to society in general, of engaging workers in the decision-making process of firms seem vague and uncertain, at least in so far as they rely upon some change in the outcome of the decisions. There may, however, be a case for participation (or co-determination) – on the grounds that, even if the decisions remained the same, welfare might be improved simply by reallocating the power of decision. This calls for a rather more general view of the process of decision-making and risk-bearing in economics, and this is taken up in the final two papers.

Aldrich examines some difficulties faced by economists when looking at anything more than the *content* of decisions. He suggests that, in analysing participation, the cost-benefit framework used by economists is rather unsuitable. He also considers the obstacles to increased participation presented by economies of scale in information processing and the need for an effective scheme of incentives.

Ingham's paper takes up the risk-sharing aspects of participation. Power and profits are the returns for taking risks, and are not free goods as implicitly assumed in some of the foregoing papers. It is argued that one may quite rationally reject industrial decision-sharing simply because the costs, in terms of risk, are too high.

There are markets for risk; and methods of trading in it are illustrated, in Ingham's paper, by examples drawn from housing, industry and agriculture. This last provides a very simple framework for describing the nature of risk and the manner of its sharing. There are three clearly defined alternatives: (*a*) pure wage contract; (*b*) crop-sharing; and (*c*) pure rent contract. These alternative arrangements offer different rewards not only in the sense that the expected returns are different, but also because the probability distributions differ. The problem is one of maximising utility under uncertainty (see Dreze [1975]) and, by making some rather strong assumptions, of deriving expressions for the trade-off between rewards which are certain and those which are not.

It turns out that the contractual arrangements between landowners and landworkers will depend upon their respective aversion to risks. Once again it seems that what is an appropriate form of participation for one group may not be appropriate for some other group which has different tastes and different endowments. On balance it might be expected that the rich would be less averse to risk than the very poor, for whom losses may be fatal. It may also be true that one section of the society has been brought up in a life style better suited to coping with large fluctuations in income. For both these reasons specialisation of risk-bearing may increase social utility. Conversely, as incomes increase, and as life styles merge, there would be a tendency for greater participation in risk-sharing and hence in the industrial decision-making processes.

Ingham indicates other duties (or social responsibilities) which were traditionally borne by those who made decisions and bore the risks in the productive activities of the community. This serves to show that risk-bearing is only one facet of a multifaceted social role, and upsetting one aspect of this role may well have other, far-reaching, social consequences. This too is illustrated with historical examples taken from agriculture.

It is hoped that this collection of papers will convey some of the flavour of the economic section of the seminar from which participants gained so much. But the principal reason for publishing this volume is the belief that it has something useful to say about a very topical subject at a time when various claims (often contradictory and sometimes little more than prejudices) are being voiced. We have tried to clarify some of the issues by constructing fairly elementary models of the industrial process, to look at some experiences of participation under socialist and capitalist systems, and finally to indicate the dangers of treating one aspect of a society as if it were isolated from others. This is indeed ambitious, and consequently we make no apology for providing only a sketchy patchwork of ideas and the most tentative of conclusions.

D.F.H.

Southampton, 1976

REFERENCES

Cole, G. D. H. [1972], *Self Government in Industry* (Hutchinson).
Cole, G. D. H. [1973], *Workshop Organization* (Hutchinson).
Domar, E. D. [1966], 'The Soviet Collective Farm as a Producer Co-operative', *American Economic Review*, 56.
Drèze J. H. [1975], 'Some Theory of Labour-Management and Participation', C.O.R.E. Discussion Paper 7520, presented at the Third World Congress of the Econometric Society, Toronto, August 1975.
Meade, J. E. [1972], 'The Theory of Labour-Managed Firms and of Profit Sharing', *Economic Journal*, 82.
Meade J. E. [1974], 'Labour Managed Firms in Conditions of Imperfect Competition', *Economic Journal*, 84.
Trades Union Congress [1974], *Industrial Democracy*.
Vanek, J. [1970], *The General Theory of Labour Managed Market Economies* (Ithaca).
Ward, B. [1958], 'The Firm in Illyria: Market Syndicalism', *American Economic Review*, 48, 4.

1 The Firm in Illyria: Market Syndicalism

Benjamin Ward[1]

The discussion of the feasibility of socialism has long been closed with apparently quite general agreement that an economy will not inevitably collapse as a result of nationalization of the means of production. On the theoretical side the clinching argument was probably made by Barone shortly after the controversy began [2]. Probably the best-known of the arguments on the other side of the question, that of Mises [15], was published twelve years after Barone's paper and gave rise to a new set of arguments, among them those of Taylor, Lange and Lerner [11] [12]. Lange in fact explicitly (though perhaps with a touch of irony) developed market socialism as a counterexample for Mises' assertions.

Today one might be inclined to take market socialism as something more than a theoretical counterexample. But as a serious proposal for social reform it leaves some important questions unanswered. For example the problem of the emergence of a bureaucracy in whose hands the economic power is largely concentrated was raised by Lange himself. Another unanswered question has to do with the behavioral response of decision-makers to such directives as the rules for determining output and changing price. Will the rules be simply obeyed or will various means of simulating compliance while serving other ends be developed?

These two questions are of special interest today as one watches some Eastern European countries groping toward a less centralized form of economic organization, and as one watches Western European socialists struggle with the implications for democracy (and efficiency) of further nationalization. In the present paper a few of the implications of one possible alternative form of industrial organization are explored. In this model the means of production are nationalized and the factories turned over to the general management of elected committees of workers who are free to set price and output policy in their own material self-interest. The nature of the resulting price and output decisions are investigated and compared with those obtained in the competitive capitalist (or market socialist) model.

The assumptions of the model bear a close resemblance to the legal status of the industrial firm in Yugoslavia in recent years. Consequently some of the organizational arrangements of a 'market syndicalist' economy can be described most conveniently by citing laws on the statute books in Yugoslavia, as is done in Section I. Toward the end of the paper some comments are made as to the extent of deviations of firm behavior in Yugoslavia from that of the theorems of our model. It seems that Illyria is in fact an alternative to the existing system in Yugoslavia as well as to those in Western and the rest of Eastern Europe.

I   LEGAL ASPECTS OF A MARKET SOCIALIST ECONOMY

The legal framework of the Yugoslav economy has been undergoing such rapid and repeated overhaul during the past seven years that it is difficult to pin down the provisions that are relevant at any one point in time. In what follows reference is mainly to the year 1954. Of first importance in releasing the firm from its former Stalinist constraints was the new planning system.[2] Federal and republican plans no longer prescribed output norms for firms and industries. Figures in the central plan represented generalized expectations rather than explicit norms. The firm itself in its own 'independent' plan set its own goals for the year and even then was not penalized for failure to fulfill these targets.

The firm was not only empowered to set its own rate of production but was also made responsible for its sales. The compulsory distribution plan was abolished [17, No. 17, 1952, item 169], and the firm was permitted to enter freely into contracts for the sale of its output and the purchase of raw materials. Prices had gradually been released from central control until here too the firm had the right to price its own products 'on the basis of market conditions.'[3] Price controls still existed in 1954 but only for a narrow range of commodities.[4]

With output norms no longer available for the purpose, the new criterion of successful performance of the firm became profitability, that is to say, the ability to earn enough in revenue to cover costs at the existing market prices. The term 'revenue' means roughly what it would mean to an American businessman. However, the term 'costs' requires some discussion in view of certain aspects of the wage system and of the fact that the state retained ownership of the means of production.

Labor cost was defined by law [17, No. 52, 1953, item 439] and was based on the average level of skill of workers in the industry. Industries were divided into eight groups on this basis and the labor cost per worker-month set for each group. For example, a coal mining concern, falling in Group III was assigned a calculated (*obračunski*) wage of 8,100 dinars per worker-month. If the firm employed a staff of 100 for a full month of work, labor cost would be 810,000 dinars for the month. The calculated wage was not the same thing as the contractual wage, which was the basis on which a worker was hired. This latter could be set freely by the firm. The distinction was that the contractual wage was not an accounting cost and was set by the firm, while the calculated wage *was* an accounting cost and was set by the state.

Secondly, there was the problem of charging the firm for its use of the state-owned land, plant and equipment. Ground rent was to be charged industrial firms at the same rate as that charged on the 'largest class of arable land in the district' [17, No. 53, 1953, item 456]. The latter was set on a cadastral basis in accord with the yield of the land. Capital, that is to say plant and equipment, including the more expensive tools, was revalued during 1953 on a basis which does not seem to have been described explicitly in the press.[5] The social (i.e., federal) plan was then to set each year the rate to be paid to the state as interest on fixed capital. A standard rate of depreciation on the various types of equipment was prescribed by the state and payments sufficient to maintain the value of the equipment were also charged as costs against the firm [16, pp. 128–32, 165–67].

Under this system then, costs would be the sum of material costs, 'regular contributions' to the state (i.e., the interest charge on fixed capital, ground rent and the excise tax on sales, where levied – a relatively insignificant item in 1954), the calculated wage fund and interest on short-term credit outstanding. Profits, i.e., revenue less costs so defined, became the measure of success of the firm.

To lend point to this change in perspective, a bankruptcy law was promulgated.[6] Several types of receivership were defined, but in general it was provided that a firm became bankrupt if it was no longer able to make its regular payments to the state and to pay wages out of its revenues at the rate guaranteed by the state.[7] Included was a provision permitting reorganization of the firm after writing down existing debts, provided the creditors were agreeable.

The new organization was designed to increase the efficiency of the economic system via competition among firms. As Vice-President Kardelj put it, ' . . . stimulative elements . . . appear above all through the interest of the enterprise in achieving, through free competition with other enterprises on the market, the best results as regards quality and quantity of goods, lower costs of production and good marketing' [10, p. 135]. The firm's incentive to participate in this competition with its fellows stemmed from two sources: workers' management and a profits-sharing scheme. The former had been established in 1950 [17, No. 43, 1950] and provided for an elected council of workers in the firm which was to serve a general policy-making function. The council approved the independent plan of the firm and the wage schedule and was empowered to issue directives regarding execution of the plan and the management of the firm. These were binding upon the firm's director, providing they did not conflict with existing laws and decrees. Day-to-day supervision of operations was entrusted to the management board (*upravni odbor*),[8] a subcommittee of the workers' council which also prepared drafts of the plan and the wage schedule for the approval of the workers' council. Differential wages within the firm were thus set by the workers themselves under this law and the later planning law, the chief constraint being that no wage rate could be set below that in the state minimum wage law.[9]

The calculated wage rates were supposed to be set at levels which would add up to 90 per cent of the total contractual wages at the planned production rate and sales price. If the workers were to recieve the contract wage then it was necessary for the firm to make a profit on its operation [1, p. 44]. Furthermore, any profits achieved by the firm were placed at the disposal of the workers' council to be used either for investment or rationalization or to be paid out as a wage supplement in proportion to the contract wage received by each worker,[10] though a steeply progressive profits tax was levied on this supplementary wage fund.

While the Yugoslav economic system thus involves a considerable measure of autonomy for the firm, it should not be thought that independence of the sort possessed within the legal framework of capitalism has been acquired by the Yugoslav firm. The state reserves the right to intervene directly to alter any decisions of which it disapproves.[11] Such intervention could occur legally as a result of new decrees of the government or by means of the exertion of influence via the trade unions, the League of Communists, or the local governments, rights whose legal sanction was often based on the right of approval of the firm's decisions.[12] But intervention was now to be viewed as the exception rather than the rule.[13]

II THE COMPETITIVE FIRM: THE ONE OUTPUT-ONE VARIABLE INPUT CASE

The Illyrian firm operates in an environment rather similar to the legal environment within which the Yugoslav firm operates. In Illyria however there will be no intervention by the state in the firm's decision-making process, nor does minimum wage legislation exist. The worker-managers are free to set firm policy under the influence of the profit incentive.

The firm to be considered in this section operates in a purely competitive market. Decision-making is concerned with the short run and is viewed as static in nature; that is, the worker-managers are interested in maximizing their individual incomes over a given period of time. The services available to the firm are labor, which is a homogeneous input, and a fixed plant, which is owned by the state and operated by the workers. The firm must pay a tax in the form of interest on the replacement cost of the plant. Ground rent, depreciation, working capital and other taxes will be ignored. The state sets the calculated wage rate w, but this is done merely to provide an accounting definition of labor cost and does not determine in fact the level of wages.[14] The workers never plough their profits back into the firm, but in each period distribute the whole amount of profits as a wage bonus. In our firm, which employs a single-skill type of worker, the distribution is made equally to each employee.

A production function will describe the technical conditions under which the firm may transform the homogeneous factor labor, x, into a salable product, y:

(1) $y = f(x).$

Over the range of the variables under consideration the marginal product of labor will be assumed to be positive but declining as output increases. Labor input will be measured in terms of the number of workers employed. By assuming that labor input can be changed only by varying the number of laborers the possibility of overtime work by the existing staff is eliminated. This is done so as to avoid introducing the marginal disutility of labor as an important constraint.[15] It is also assumed that there is no discrimination among workers, and that a decision to lay off workers on profit-maximizing grounds would not be affected by the fact that the result would be to create unemployment.[16]

The sole source of income to the firm is from the sale of its product at the parametric price p. Two costs are incurred in production: labor cost which is valued at the calculated wage w per worker,[17] and the fixed charge for the use of capital R. Profit of course is the difference between revenue and cost. The worker-managers, acting in their own material self-interest, are not necessarily interested in maximizing profits as their capitalist counterparts, the stockholders or entrepreneurs, would be. Each worker is interested in maximizing his own wage income. The workers as a group, corresponding to the group of stock-holders in capitalism, are interested in adopting policies which will maximize

(2) $S = w + \dfrac{\pi}{x}$

where π represents profits.

The last term of equation (2) can be divided into two parts since average profits per worker consists of the difference between average revenue per worker, U, and average cost per worker, K. The firm will then choose that output which will make the positive difference between U and K a maximum. This would be the output at which

(3) $dU/dy = dK/dy.$

This is the Illyrian equivalent of the capitalist condition that price will equal marginal cost under rational management, or of the market socialist rule that managers act so as to set marginal cost equal to price. The Illyrian condition states that wages per worker (or, what amounts to the same thing, profits per worker) are maximized if the competitive firm chooses the output at which marginal revenue-per-worker equals marginal cost-per-worker.[18] This condition has more in common with the capitalist 'rule' than with the Lange-Lerner rule. For the Illyrian rule represents the *result* of behavior of a specified kind (wage-maximizing behavior), as does the neoclassical rule (profit-maximizing behavior). In the market socialist economy of the Lange-Lerner type however, the managers are *directed* by the state to act in a certain way, the rule not being connected explicitly with the motivations of the managers.

Equilibrium for the Illyrian competitive firm is described graphically in Figure 1.1, where the values of U and K are plotted against x. The solution is not altered by making x rather than y the formal choice variable. U has its maximum value at the point at which marginal and average product are equal[19] and declines as the number of workers is either increased or decreased from this value. K, representing average costs per worker, is equal to

$$w + \frac{R}{x}$$

This curve is a rectangular hyperbola asymptotic to $x = 0$, $K = w$. Profits per worker reach a maximum when the difference between U and K is greatest, which is the value of x for which the slopes of U and K are equal. This is point b of Figure 1.1.

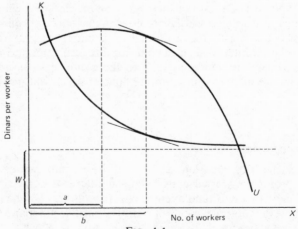

Fig. 1.1

What is the meaning of this equilibrium? How does it compare with the equilibrium position of the traditional firm? We may consider first the effects of changes in the parameters on the Illyrian firm's behavior, and then contrast the equilibrium positions of Illyrian and capitalist firms under similar technological and market conditions.

Referring to Figure 1.2, suppose that the firm is in equilibrium producing, under revenue and cost conditions represented by U_1 and K_1 an output corresponding to the level of employment a. The state now raises the interest rate, so that R is increased. This shifts the cost curve up to K_2. But at the output corresponding to a, curve K_2 is steeper than is U_1.[26] That is to say, at employment level a the rate of decrease of average cost per worker is greater than the rate of decrease of average revenue per worker. Consequently it will be to the workers' advantage to raise output until average cost and average revenue per worker are decreasing at the same rate. In Figure 1.2 this is represented by employment level b where the slopes of U_1 and K_2 are equal. This result can be generalized into the theorem: *A change in the fixed costs of the competitive Illyrian firm leads to a change in output in the same direction.*

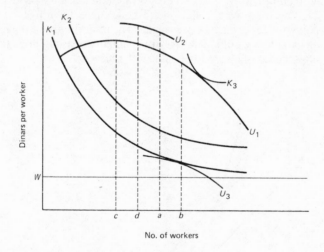

FIG. 1.2

Further increases in R would lead to further increases in output. If K_3 were the relevant cost curve the firm would be earning zero profits. Even if R were increased beyond this point output would continue to increase, as the worker-managers strove to minimize losses. Under these circumstances the workers would be receiving less than the calculated wage w. So long as no better alternatives were available elsewhere the workers would continue to work in the given firm despite this fact, under our assumptions.[21] Decreases in R of course have the opposite effect. At $R = 0$, the cost function becomes $K_4 = w$, and output would be at the level corresponding to the maximum value of U_1. A negative interest rate would convert K into a hyperbola asymptotic to the same lines as before but located below w on Figure 1.2. Employment would be less than c and the competitive Illyrian firm would be in equilibrium with average costs falling.[22]

Price changes may be considered in a similar way. Suppose that an increase in demand for the industry's product leads to an increase in the market price p of our firm, which is currently in equilibrium at employment level a of Figure 1.2. This will shift U_1 upwards to position U_2. But at the current employment level U_2 will be steeper than K_1.[23] That is, at a the rate of decrease of average revenue per worker is greater than the rate of decrease of average cost per worker. Output and employment will contract until these rates are again equal as at employment level d. Our theorem is: *A change in price to the competitive Illyrian firm leads to a change in output in the opposite direction.*

The lower limit to a price-induced output contraction is, roughly speaking, at employment level c where average and marginal product are equal. If falling price were to shift the revenue curve down to U_3 a zero profits position would have been reached. The remarks above regarding operations at a loss would of course apply equally if falling price rather than rising fixed costs were the cause of the losses.[24]

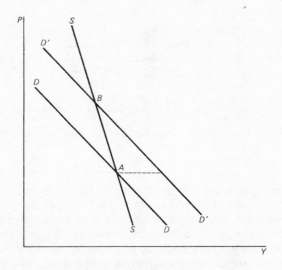

FIG. 1.3

Under the usually hypothesized market and technological conditions the Illyrian competitive firm possesses a negatively sloped supply curve. This does not mean however that Illyrian competitive markets are inherently unstable. For example, Figure 1.3 depicts the industry supply and demand curves in such a market. If demand were to shift from DD to $D'D'$ point A would no longer be an equilibrium position. If this is a 'price-adjusting' market in the usual sense, the adjusting mechanism is such that the direction of movement of price over time has the same sign as the amount of excess demand. In the diagram excess demand is now positive, so price increases and eventually equilibrium is restored.

On the other hand, if the demand curve has a steeper slope than the supply curve the adjusting mechanism described above will lead away from equilibrium and the market will be unstable. To be assured of stability this possibility must be avoided, which means that some further constraint must be imposed on the structure of the firm specified above.[25] The problem of instability is most likely to arise when product demand is relatively inelastic, or when marginal product is relatively large and declining slowly as output increases.

If the state changes the calculated wage w there is no change in any of the variables relevant to the firm. The K function (*cf.* Figure 1.1) shifts vertically up or down as a result. The income of the workers is unchanged, though relatively more income is in the form of profits (if w is reduced) and relatively less in the form of wages.[26]

The Illyrian equilibrium can now be contrasted with its capitalist counterpart. Consider two firms, one in Illyria, the other in a capitalist country. They have identical production functions and are operating in purely competitive markets. In addition, market prices are equal in both cases, as are fixed costs, and the Illyrian calculated wage w_I equals the going capitalist wage w_C. In Figure 1.4 the U and K functions describe the revenue and cost positions of the Illyrian firm under alternative levels of employment. The rates of change are also drawn in. At the intersection of the latter the Illyrian firm is in equilibrium, producing the output corresponding to employment x_I.

In describing the equilibrium of the capitalist firm it will first be noted that U also expresses the value of the average product of the capitalist firm under our assumptions, since $U = py/x$. The capitalist value-of-the-marginal-product function bears the usual relation to U, and the capitalist output is found at the point x_C where VMP equals the wage, since output y_C is a single-valued function of labor input.[27]

In the diagram the capitalist output exceeds that of the Illyrian firm. But this need not be the case. For example, by increasing w_C it would be possible to reduce the equilibrium output level of this firm to the Illyrian level or even below. Under our assumptions a necessary and sufficient condition that the outputs of the two firms be equal is that the equilibrium marginal products be equal. The capitalist value of the marginal product is equal to w_C. In Illyria the value of the marginal product is equal to the 'full' wage, *i.e.*, the calculated wage plus the profits share to each worker.[28] Therefore the Illyrian full wage equals the capitalist wage and equality of outputs implies zero profits.[29]

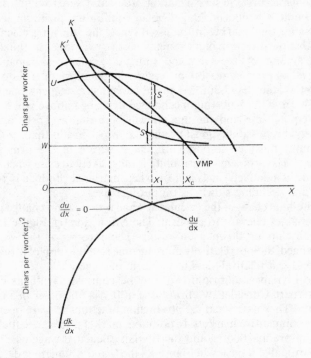

FIG. 1.4

Thus the Illyrian firm is capable of producing in the short run at a level equal to or even greater than that of its capitalist counterpart. And the state can affect output decisions of the firm via its ability to alter the parameter R. If it is willing to use the fixed tax for capital use as an instrument of policy in attaining desired levels of output, and consequently is willing to make discriminatory charges on this basis, it may create an environment in which it is in the material interests of the worker-managers to produce at the competitive capitalist output, or at some other preferred rate. Alternatively, if the industry were in long-run equilibrium in both countries and demand, labor force, etc., conditions were identical, both firms would produce the same output.

Finally, the case of constant average product y/x may be noted. In capitalism this means one of three things: (1) if $VMP > w$ the firm produces at capacity; (2) if $VMP < w$ the firm produces nothing; and

(3) if $VMP = w$ output is indeterminate. In the Illyrian case this means that U is a horizontal line. The maximum positive, or minimum negative, difference between U and K consequently is at infinity whatever the position of U on the diagram. The Illyrian firm produces at capacity when marginal and average product are equal.

III　THE CASE OF TWO VARIABLE INPUTS

In Illyria a single class of inputs, labor, is singled out for special treatment. The distinctive features of Illyrian behavior stem entirely from this fact. By extending our previous model to include the use by the firm of a variable nonlabor input, the special position of labor in the firm can be brought out more clearly. The production function will now have the two arguments,

$$(6) \qquad y = f(x, z).$$

If the usual assumptions of positive marginal products and diminishing returns to the factors are made, the equilibrium condition for labor use will correspond to that in Section II, i.e., the value of the marginal product of labor will be equal to the full wage. For the nonlabor input however the value of the marginal product will be equal to the price v of the input.[30] The workers react to changes in nonlabor inputs in the same manner as do capitalists: they will increase their use of the factor as long as it contributes more to revenue than to cost. On the other hand they seem to use a different criterion in evaluating labor use. An additional laborer must contribute more to revenue per worker than to cost per worker in order for him to be employed. In fact, *only* the latter criterion is being employed in the model. It simply happens that the capitalist and Illyrian criteria lead to the same behavior with regard to nonlabor inputs. Whenever one of these factors contributes more to revenue than to cost it also contributes more to revenue per worker than to cost per worker. As a result the equilibrium conditions are the same. However the two criteria do not lead to the same behavior when it comes to labor use. Because each laborer gets a share of the profits it does not follow that an additional worker who contributes more to revenue than to cost will necessarily also contribute more to revenue per worker than to cost per worker. As a result the equilibrium conditions for labor use are not the same in the two regimes.

　　An analysis of the effects of changes in the parameters R and p leads to less clear results in the two-input case than it did in Section II: In the case of a change in fixed costs the analysis may be illustrated by means of the factor allocation diagrams of Figure 1.5. The curves in 5A are drawn on the assumption of a fixed input of factor z and those in 5B on the

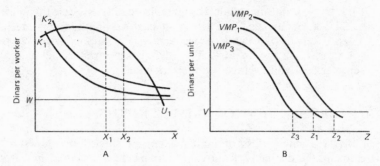

FIG. 1.5

assumption of a fixed level of employment. From an initial position of equilibrium in which x_1 of x and z_1 of z are being used, fixed cost is increased. This shifts K_1 upward to K_2, increasing labor input from x_1 to x_2, and consequently tending to increase output. However, there is now an additional effect which must be taken into account: namely the effect of the increase in labor use on the marginal product of the nonlabor input. If the latter is unaffected or increases, shifting VMP_1 upwards to VMP_2, the increase in output is either unaffected or magnified. However, if VMP is reduced by the increased labor use the amount of z used decreases, and the output effect of the increase in fixed cost is indeterminate by means of qualitative analysis alone. The latter, however, is a rather unlikely eventuality, since in the short run more labor will generally not decrease the usefulness of the other variable factors, and conversely. Consequently a change in fixed cost in the multifactor case will also tend to lead to a change in output in the same direction.

A more serious indeterminacy appears in the analysis of price changes. Without a good deal more information it is not possible to state the effect on output of a change in price. The possibility of a positively inclined supply curve emerges clearly however, and some presumption that the danger of instability, resulting from a negatively inclined and relatively elastic supply curve, has diminished. Whether or not a negatively sloped supply curve will result in the multifactor case depends on the relative importance of labor in the bill of inputs.[31] Similarly, changes in the parameter v, the supply price of the non-labor input z, have indeterminate effects on output. This is also true in the case of analysis of the capitalist firm with the same amount of information, though information sufficient to remove the indeterminacy in one case may not be sufficient in the other.

The statements made in Section I comparing competitive capitalism with competition in Illyria generally apply in the somewhat more complicated two-variable-input case. We will consider here the problem of comparative factor allocation. As before our two firms have identical production functions and are operating under identical market conditions so that:

$$p^I = p^C$$
$$w^I = w^C$$
$$v^I = v^C$$
$$R^I = R^C$$

the superscripts standing for 'Illyria' and 'Capitalism' respectively.

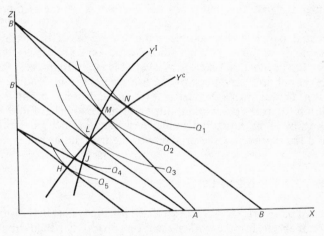

FIG. 1.6

The situation is described in Figure 1.6 in which isoquants Q_i which are identical for both firms are drawn. Let us assume first that the capitalist firm is producing output Q_1. BB is the factor-cost line based on the values of w and v, so that the capitalist firm is in equilibrium at a factor mix represented by point N. Let us assume further that the capitalist firm is earning a profit at this level of operation. At the same output the Illyrian firm would be earning a profit too. But it would not be in equilibrium at point N. This is because BB is not the relevant factor cost line for the Illyrian firm. Since in Illyria the value of the marginal product of labor is equated to the full wage, i.e., including the profits share, BA, representing a larger wage 'cost', is the relevant one for the Illyrian allocation decision. The Illyrian firm is in equilibrium then at point M, producing less output and using less labor than its capitalist counterpart.

Suppose now that market price falls to the zero profits point. Capitalist output and factor mix contract along Y^C, say to point L. Illyrian output and factor mix contract along Y^I, but also to point L, since the zero-profits full wage is equal to w. If price should fall further so that both firms are incurring losses the full wage will then be less than w. For example, under conditions which would lead the capitalist firm to produce at H, the Illyrian firm would produce at J. The Illyrian firm would produce more than the capitalist firm and would use more labor, so as to spread the losses around among as many of the worker-managers as possible.

The Y^I line, like Y^C, is positively sloped in the diagram, indicating that supply responds positively to an increase in price. It is perfectly possible for Y^I to have a negative slope under suitable cost and technological conditions, but it will still intersect Y^C at the zero-profits point. [32]

As a final aspect of the multiple-input case we may consider a firm which is highly automated so that labor does not enter significantly into the short-run production function as a variable input. In this case factor use and output are determined by the usual equilibrium conditions of capitalism. That is, with a fixed labor force any addition to profits is also an addition to profits per worker. Such a firm would behave in exactly the same way as its capitalist counterpart, equating marginal cost to price and the marginal value products to the fixed input prices.

IV   MARKET IMPERFECTIONS

Illyria must pay a price for its decentralized pricing system in the form of imperfect markets. For the worker-managers no less than their capitalist counterparts have an incentive to profit from the negatively inclined demand schedule that must in many instances confront them. The whole congeries of market types from monopoly to monopolistic competition, including the usual forms of collusion, could emerge under Illyrian conditions. Alterations in the previous models required to take account of such market imperfections in most instances are not extensive. For example, the monopoly solution in the single-variable-input case can be discussed by means of Figure 1.2 (p. 574) if the U function is reinterpreted to take account of the fact that price is now a variable rather than a parameter of the system. That is, any point on U would now represent the average revenue that would accrue to the monopoly from selling the output the x workers are capable of producing at the price offered for that quantity by buyers. The result is that factors are used up to the point at which the marginal revenue product equals the (assumed perfectly elastic) supply price in the case of nonlabor inputs, and to the point at which marginal revenue product equals the 'full' wage for labor inputs.[33] Output will be less than in competition under the usual conditions.

There is one factor market which exhibits a special rigidity in Illyria; namely the labor market. The situation can be illustrated by assuming away all the customary forms of rigidity in the labor market such as trade unions, barriers to training, imperfect knowledge, etc. If labor is a homogeneous factor well informed and concerned to better its material position as far as possible, we may assume the supply to depend solely on the wage offered. If profits figures are published or otherwise available it is the full wage that will determine the offer of labor power. Suppose that from an initial position of equilibrium the supply schedule for labor shifts up, leading to excess demand. Ignoring the influence of varying employment levels on product demand, the marginal firms are now unable to obtain labor at the going wage rate. But they are also unable to offer higher wages, since the wage rate was already at a maximum. As a result of the rigidity of the wage offer there will be no forces set in motion in the short run to correct a disequilibrium, and the shortage of workers will in itself tend to depress the wage paid by the marginal firms, since profits can no longer be maximized.

If excess supply of labor should develop, a similar rigidity would occur. Workers are willing to offer themselves at lower wage rates, but these rates cannot legally be paid. Consequently the excess supply will persist. Only entry or departure by some firms would be capable of changing the situation; i.e., by changes in the quantities demanded in each case rather than by alterations in the market price of labor.

If profit rates were kept secret it might be possible to create a supply function in which the nominal wage w_1 was the independent variable. In this case, when excess demand appeared the state could raise the nominal rate sufficiently to attract the needed number of workers into the market. This change in the wage would not affect the full wage or the product market positions.[34] That is, it would affect only the supply of labor, not the demand. However it would be rather difficult to keep all information regarding profits from the labor market when all recipients of profits or losses were also workers.

V CONCLUDING REMARKS

1. The zero-profit output of the competitive Illyrian and competitive capitalist firms will be identical, given the same market and technological conditions for the two firms. This suggests that in the long run the Illyrian conditions under competition could lead to an optimal allocation of resources wherever the capitalist regime would. However we have not discussed conditions of entry in Illyria. Entry could occur either by creation of new firms by the state, or by expansion of existing

firms, or by some provision for individual or decentralized group initiative in starting new enterprises. All three possibilities exist in Yugoslavia but it is not possible to discuss them here. It will merely be noted that there is likely to be strong resistance by the Illyrian worker-managers to ploughing back profits, since this would involve a reduction in the current profits share. This will be true if relatively low-income entrepreneurs are likely to be more myopic than relatively high-income ones. Something additional to worker self interest might well be necessary in the Illyrian environment to ensure entry equivalent to that under capitalism.

2. Market imperfections stemming from the ability of the seller (or buyer) to influence the market price by varying his rate of output lead generally to a lower level of output and a higher price than the competitive rates, in Illyria as in capitalism. This has been a persistent problem in Yugoslavia from the beginning of the new system [7, p. 16] [4, 1953, 2, 443–44] [4, 1954, 3, 841–42] and has led to the promulgation of an 'antitrust' law.[35] The state's broad rights of intervention might seem to offer more favourable opportunities for controlling such behavior, but persistent complaints in the Yugoslav press suggest that control of monopoly has not been notably success-ful.[36] Of course Yugoslavia, being a rather small country with an underdeveloped industrial sector and communications network, and with a balance-of-payments problem which has led to a large number of restrictions on competitive imports, has considerable initial disadvantages to overcome in developing a purely competitive market.

3. A special stability problem arises in Illyria, since firms may react to a price change by altering the rate of output in the opposite direction (negatively sloped supply schedule), a situation which is more likely to occur the more important labor is as an input. Since a good deal of new plant has been installed in Yugoslavia since 1952, this would be a difficult hypothesis to test. Indeed, our model does not tell us anything at all about what to expect if there is in fact instability in a market. In addition it is possible that in a large number of Yugoslav firms policy decisions are made by the director without much reference to the wage-maximizing desires of the workers. Though directors also share in the profits, it is likely that other motives also exist for them which might lead to different behavior as regards price and output and input policy.[37]

4. The beginning student of economics would undoubtedly be delighted to learn that in Illyria an increase in fixed costs would really lead to an increase in output so as to spread out the increased burden over a larger number of units. I have seen no evidence to indicate that the Yugoslav authorities have varied the interest rate on existing capital for purposes of output control, though discrimination has been practiced which is consistent with such an aim.[38]

5. The labor market possesses a rigidity which prevents adjustment of

supply and demand to restore a displacement from equilibrium. It is true that in Yugoslavia there has been some excess supply of labor at least since the institution of the new economic system in 1952 [4, 1953, *2*, 182–83] [9], though this can be explained as well by other factors operating generally in a labor market in an underdeveloped country (and by the successive droughts) as by means of this theorem. In this excess-supply situation some incentive probably exists for the firm to practice a form of illegal discrimination which *is* related to the specific rigidity described above. This could be done by means of illegal contract to hire workers who would agree to work for the contractual wage rate for unskilled workers and renounce their right to profits.[39]

Finally, outside pressure by various groups, but especially by the people's committees, the organs of local government, seems to have had considerable effect on decision-making by the firm in Yugoslavia. We will note only one example. The people's committees possess the right to a portion of the profits of every firm within their territory. This has led them to influence the firms' policies and to take other steps to siphon funds from the firms into the treasury of the local government.[40] The actions of local governments and other administrative bodies, plus fears of administrative intervention, undoubtedly result in significant differences in the behavior of firms in Yugoslavia and Illyria. These factors, plus the relatively large role the director seems to play in *de facto* decision-making within the Yugoslav firm, provide the chief limitations to application of the above analysis to current operations in Yugoslavia. The model's relevance to Yugoslavia may be somewhat increased if it is assumed that the legal framework is descriptive of an ultimate purpose on the part of the Yugoslav leadership.

In summary, market syndicalism differs from market socialism in that in the former (1) both price and output decisions are decentralized to the level of the firm; (2) the workers employed in each firm control policy making; and (3) material interest is the governing incentive. Some of the arguments in favor of market syndicalism as a non-bureaucratic alternative to other forms of socialism would bear a striking resemblance to those of the economic liberal when attacking some tendencies of contemporary capitalism; and conversely for arguments against market syndicalism. However it would not be seemly to discuss these issues until some other properties of the Illyrian economy, such as the investment decision, multiple market stability and macroeconomics, have been investigated.

MATHEMATICAL APPENDIX

1. *The Condition for Stability in a Single Competitive Illyrian Market under the Assumptions of Section II.*

From equations (2) and (3) in the text

(7)
$$S = \frac{py}{x} - w - \frac{R}{x}$$

so that

(8)
$$\frac{dS}{dy} = \frac{p(x - yx') + Rx'}{x^2} = 0$$

where $x' \equiv dx/dy$. The equilibrium condition $S' = px - pyx' + Rx' = 0$ may be differentiated with respect to the parameter p:

$$\frac{\partial S'}{\partial p}\bigg|_R = \frac{dS'\partial y}{dy\,\partial p}\bigg|_R + \frac{\partial S'}{\partial p}\bigg|_{y,\,R} \equiv 0$$

$$= (-pyx'' + Rx'')(\partial y/\partial p) + (x - yx') \equiv 0$$

or the slope of the firm's supply function:

(9)
$$\frac{\partial y}{\partial p} = \frac{yx' - x}{x''(R - py)}.$$

But $(R - py) = -pxy'$, since the equilibrium is preserved along the supply function. So supply elasticity:

(10)
$$\eta s \equiv \frac{p\partial y}{y\partial p} = \frac{x'}{xx''}\left(\frac{x}{y} - x'\right) < 0,$$

except over the relatively unimportant range in which average product is equal to or less than marginal product. Note that

$$x'' \equiv \frac{d^2x}{dy^2} = \frac{y''}{(-y')^3} > 0, \quad \text{where} \quad y'' \equiv \frac{d^2y}{dx^2}.$$

We are assuming a price-adjusting market in which the existence of excess demand leads to price increases over time in the case of excess demand and of decreases in the case of excess supply. Such a market will be stable when the supply curve is negatively sloped provided $\eta_D > \eta_S$. If we assume that production functions of all firms are identical, elasticity is invariant under the summation from firm to industry supply function. Thinking then in terms of industry demand and firm supply conditions, we have:

$$(11) \qquad \eta_D > \eta_S = \frac{x'}{xx''}\left(\frac{x}{y} - x'\right)$$

as a necessary and sufficient condition for stability.

2. Monopoly with One Variable Input.

Equation (7) applies in this case, except that p is now a variable. Assume

$$(12) \qquad p = g(y, \alpha)$$

such that $\partial p/\partial y < 0$ and α, a shift parameter, is defined so that $\partial p/\partial \alpha > 0$ and further that $\partial p/\partial y$ remains invariant under the shift. Differentiating (7) with respect to y and solving for the first order condition for a maximum ($y' \equiv 1/x'$):

$$(13) \qquad y'(p + p'y) = (py - R)/x, \text{ where } p' = \frac{\partial p}{\partial y}\bigg|_{\alpha}$$

Equation (13) may be differentiated with respect to R and α, respectively, and solved for:

$$\frac{\partial y}{\partial R} = -\frac{x'}{2p'x + p''xy - x''(py - R)}$$

and

$$\frac{\partial y}{\partial \alpha} = \frac{(\partial p/\partial \alpha)(x'y - x) - xy\left(\dfrac{\partial^2 p}{\partial y \partial \alpha}\right)}{2p'x + p''xy - x''(py - R)}.$$

Knowledge of signs tells us that, as long as the demand curve is linear or convex to the origin, a change in R leads to a change in y in the same direction. With a similar demand curve, an upward shift in demand of the hypothesized kind will lead to a decrease in output if the firm is operating beyond the point of maximum average product, but an increase in output if average product is still increasing.

3. The Two-Variable-Input Case.

$$(14) \qquad S = \frac{1}{x}\left[py - (wx + vz + R)\right]$$

and

(15)
$$y = f(x, z), \quad y_x > 0, \quad y_z > 0,$$
$$y_{xx} < 0, \quad y_{zz} < 0, \quad \text{and} \quad y_{xx}y_{zz} - y_{xz}^2 > 0.$$

Applying the first-order conditions for a maximum,

(16) $\partial S/\partial x = (1/x^2)[p(xy_x - y) + vz + R] = 0$

and

(17) $\partial S/\partial z = (1/x)(py_z - v) = 0$

or

(18) $py_x = \dfrac{py - (vz + R)}{x}$

and

(19) $py_z = v.$

Further differentiation of (16) and (17) gives, at the equilibrium position at which (18) and (19) are satisfied,

$$\partial^2 S/\partial x^2 = py_{xx}/x < 0,$$
$$\partial^2 S/\partial z^2 = py_{zz}/x < 0,$$
$$\partial^2 S/\partial x \partial z = py_{xz}/x$$

and

$$\frac{\partial^2 S}{\partial x^2}\frac{\partial^2 S}{\partial z^2} - \left(\frac{\partial^2 S}{\partial x \partial z}\right)^2 = \frac{p^2}{x^2}(y_{xx}y_{zz} - y_{xz}^2) > 0.$$

Therefore equations (18) and (19) determine a maximum. Both the latter equations can be differentiated with respect to R and with respect to p and solved for:

$$\frac{\partial x}{\partial R} = \frac{\begin{vmatrix} -1 & (pxy_{xz}) \\ 0 & (py_{zz}) \end{vmatrix}}{p^2 x \begin{vmatrix} y_{xx} & y_{xz} \\ y_{xz} & y_{zz} \end{vmatrix}} > 0,$$

$$\frac{\partial z}{\partial R} = \frac{\begin{vmatrix} (pxy_{x\,x}) & -1 \\ (py_{xz}) & 0 \end{vmatrix}}{p^2 x \begin{vmatrix} y_{x\,x} & y_{xz} \\ y_{xz} & y_{zz} \end{vmatrix}} \gtrless 0,$$

$$\frac{\partial x}{\partial p} = \frac{\begin{vmatrix} (y - xy_x) & (pxy_{xz}) \\ (-y_z) & (py_{zz}) \end{vmatrix}}{p^2 x \begin{vmatrix} y_{x\,x} & y_{xz} \\ y_{xz} & y_{zz} \end{vmatrix}} \gtrless 0$$

$$\frac{\partial z}{\partial p} = \frac{\begin{vmatrix} (pxy_{x\,x}) & (y - xy_x) \\ (py_{xz}) & (-y_z) \end{vmatrix}}{p^2 x \begin{vmatrix} y_{x\,x} & y_{xz} \\ y_{xz} & y_{zz} \end{vmatrix}} \gtrless 0.$$

The slope of the supply function at the equilibrium point,

$$\frac{\partial y}{\partial p} = y_x \frac{\partial x}{\partial p} + y_z \frac{\partial z}{\partial p}$$

$$(20) \qquad = \frac{\left[y_{zz} y_x (y - xy_x) - x y_z^2 y_{x\,x} + y_{xz}(xy_x y_z - yy_z + xy_x) \right]}{px(y_{x\,x} y_{zz} - y_{xz}^2)} \gtrless 0.$$

The denominator is positive, but the numerator is undetermined in sign with the specified information.

NOTES

1. The author would like to thank Gustavo, Escobar, Eberhard Fels, Arthur Goldberger, Gregory Grossman and Andreas Papandreou for critical comment on this paper, without committing them to any of the argument.
2. [17, No. 58, 1951]. The 1954 plan is published in [17, No. 13, 1954, item 146].
3. This had been carried out for certain classes of firms and industries during 1950–5 (for example price-setting in the case of textile products by the price bureaus of the Ministry for Domestic Trade was abolished by a decree published in [17, No. 48, 1951, item 454]). The general statute appears in [17, No. 32, 1952, item 382].
4. Prices of some industrial raw materials (e.g., pig and cast iron and sawn timber) were fixed by decree during 1954 [17, No. 20, item 221; No. 26, item 295; No. 32, item 407]. The Federal Price Office was re-established early in 1955 [17, No. 22, 1955, item 225] but there was no signficant increase in the number of controlled prices at the time.
5. D. Misić [14] says that capital was to be valued at its 'real present value, taking

account both of its economic obsolescence and the extent to which it is worn out.'
6. [17, No. 51, 1953, item 425]. An earlier law [17, No. 57, 1951, item 545] is much less specific and does not define the conditions under which a decree of bankruptcy against a firm will be passed.
7. In 1954 the state guaranteed up to 80 per cent of the calculated wage fund of the firm. A firm could apply to the state bank for a loan to cover up to 90 per cent of this fund, but the bank could refuse the loan if it thought the chances of repayment were not good. Guarantee of the loan by the local government (*narodni obdor* or 'people's committee') was often required [17, No. 5, 1954, item 57].
8. The director was a member *ex officio* of the management board.
9. [17, No. 7, 1952, item 108] [17, No. 56, 1953, item 484]. Worker skills were classified in [17, No. 57, 1950, item 508], and minimum compensation fixed for each grade.
10. There are several qualifications to this statement. Some portion of the profits was to be used for the building up of a reserve fund and the local government received a share as well [1, p. 44].
11. An official statement in vindication of the use of this right by Vice-President Kardelj can be found in [10, p. 133].
12. The people's committee had the right of approval of the firm's independent plan (see planning law cited above, footnote 1) and the trade unions had some special rights of intervention in the hire-fire decision [17, No. 26, 1952, item 306].
13. Such action is termed "administrative intervention" by Yugoslav economists and is asserted to have been ubiquitous under the previous Stalinist form of economic organization. A principal reason for establishing the new system was to make such actions unnecessary. See for example [13, pp. 95–100, 113 ff., 131–32, 224 ff.] [18, pp. 238 ff.].
14. In Yugoslavia the setting of the calculated wage performs an important function in determining the portion of the firm's wage bill that comes under the progressive surplus profits tax but we are ignoring this tax in the Illyrian case.
15. The Yugoslav wage law cited above provides that time-and-a-half be paid for overtime work, but that such work cannot be paid for unless prior authorization has been obtained from the local government. Apparently there was a tendency to hog the work which, reasonably enough, was frowned upon by the authorities in a labor surplus economy.
16. The management board has the final decision in the matter of hiring and firing in the Yugoslav firm (with the exception noted above, fn. 11). If it is assumed that the board is composed of workers of relatively long tenure in their employment in the firm, so that they would not be personally affected by a decision to reduce output, aside from the favorable effect on their own income, this assumption may seem reasonable.
17. All workers and employees, including those whose wage cost to the firm would ordinarily be considered as overhead, are included in the wage cost wx, as a matter of convenience.
18. Marginal revenue-per-worker, it will be noticed, is not the same thing as marginal revenue per worker. The former measures the change in average revenue per worker brought about by a small change in output, while the latter measures the average marginal revenue per worker. In symbols, marginal revenue-per-worker is:

$$\frac{d(py/x)}{dy} = p.\frac{x - yx'}{x^2}$$

while marginal revenue per worker is:

$$\frac{d(py)/dy}{x} = \frac{p}{x}.$$

19. From the preceding footnote it can be seen that marginal revenue-per-worker will be

zero when x/y equals x'. The shape of the production function ensures that this will be a maximum value for U.

20. Since $K = w + (R/x)$, $dK/dx = -R/x^2$. Therefore, if $R_2 > R_1 |dK_2/dx| > |dK_1/dx|$ at $x = a$.

21. In Yugoslavia wages up to 80 per cent of the calculated wage are guaranteed by the government. If this were true of Illyria, then at outputs beyond that which yielded $0.8w$ to the workers the maximization criterion would cease to apply. Continued operation at such a level would eventually lead to bankruptcy.

22. As in capitalism this would only be true over the range in which marginal product was declining. Beyond that range the second-order condition for equilibrium would not be satisfied, so that if a solution existed it would not be a maximum. It may also be noted that over this range of values the supply curve would be positively sloped.

23. $dU/dx = (p/x)[y' - (y/x)]$. Hence if $p_2 > p_1$ then $|dU_2/dx| > |dU_1/dx|$ at $x = a$.

24. The effects of changes in p and R can perhaps be seen more clearly by considering the equilibrium condition:

(4)
$$\frac{dS}{dx} = \frac{p(xy' - y) + R}{x^2} = 0$$

or

(5)
$$\frac{y}{x} - y' = \frac{R}{px}.$$

Thus the right-hand term of (5) measures the difference between average and marginal product in equilibrium, which will be positive (decreasing average product) if R is positive. But the difference between average and marginal product is a monotonic increasing function of output beyond the point of maximum average product (at which point the difference is nil). So, from equation (5), if R is increased the difference between average and marginal product, and hence equilibrium output, will be increased. On the other hand an increase in p means a decrease in the difference between average and marginal product, and hence a decrease in equilibrium output.

25. See the Mathematical Appendix.

26. See note 14 above.

27. We are assuming that the capitalist firm too can vary only the number of workers employed and not the hours of work.

28. From equations (2) and (5), $S = (py - R)/x = py'$ in equilibrium.

29. We assumed at the start that $w_I = w_C$. Since the value of w_I really does not make any difference, a more significant statement would be: equality of outputs implies equal wages.

30. See the Mathematical Appendix for derivations in the two-variable-input case.

31. *Cf.* equation (20) in the Appendix.

32. Figure 6 may also be used to contrast other comparative static changes. For example, an increase in w will increase the slope of BB without affecting that of BA. This will tend to move the capitalist equilibrium position at N closer to the Illyrian at M. An increase in R on the other hand will tend to make BA less steep without affecting the slope of BB. This will tend to move the Illyrian equilibrium position at M closer to the capitalist at N. When the equilibria coincide in either case profits will be zero.

33. See Appendix, note 2.

34. However, with a progressive profits tax, as exists in Yugoslavia, the full wage will be reduced, *ceteris paribus*, by a decrease in w, since a larger proportion of the wage bill would become taxable; and of course the full wage would increase with an increase in the calculated wage.

35. [17, No. 56, 1953, item 483, esp. Article 74]. The language is fully as vague as that of the Sherman Act, among other things forbidding firms from doing anything which leads to a 'monopoly position in the market'.
36. See however [4, 1953, 2, 1034] for a description of the refusal of a Yugoslav court to uphold a contract which was in restraint of trade.
37. See [19] for a discussion of the relative influence of director, management board and workers' council within the firm. For example, directors are often in close contact with local government officials. One possible result of ties of this kind might be profit-maximizing behavior, as mentioned in note 38 below.
38. [16, pp. 132–33]. In the 1954 plan, for example, the standard rate was 6 per cent, but in some types of construction no interest at all was charged, while elsewhere a rate of 2 per cent was charged. It is certainly true that the state was specially interested in increasing output in the favored areas. It does not necessarily follow however that the planners had the mechanism operative in our model in mind in granting the favors.
39. A phenomenon known as the "dead brigades" (*mrtvi brigadi*) may have been an instance of this [4, 1953, 2, 1034] [9, p. 487]. For example the coal mining concern mentioned on p. 568 above might hire an unskilled worker for 6000 dinars per month, which would add 8100 dinars to the calculated wage fund, i.e., to labor cost in the accounting sense. This would substantially reduce accounting profits and hence the amount of taxation under the steeply progressive profits tax law. If the firm expected to make a fairly high level of profits, this could be to the monetary advantage of the 'in-group' workers even if the newly hired worker performed no work at all. From the above descriptions it seems that the dead brigades in fact had little to do. In some cases the dead brigades were in fact 'dead souls', fictitious employees.
40. [8, p. 159] [5]. The people's committee would be interested in the level of profits per se, rather than in profits per worker, so that within the framework of our model such disagreements over price-output policy could arise.

REFERENCES

1. A. Adašević (ed.), *Novi privredni propisi* [The new economic decrees] (Belgrade, 1954).
2. E. Barone, 'P. ministerio della produzione nello stato collettivista', *Gior. d. Econ.* (1908); English translation in reference 6.
3. B. P. Beckwith, *The Economic Theory of a Socialist Economy* (Stanford, Calif., 1949) Bibliography, pp. 433–5.
4. *Ekonomska politika* [Economic Policy] Belgrade (weekly), 1952.
5. S. Gligorijević, 'Zapazanja iz rada komunista u industriskim preduzećima' [Observations on the Work of Communists in Industrial Firms], *Komunist*, 4, 7 (1955) 243–7.
6. F. A. von Hayek, ed., *Collectivist Economic Planning* (London, 1935).
7. B. Iovanović, 'Iskustva iz primene novog privrednog sistema' [Experience with the Operation of the New Economic System], *Ekonomist*, 4, 5 (1952) 12–22.
8. E. Kardelj, 'O nekim nedostacima u radu komunista'[Certain

Shortcomings in the Work of Communists], *Komunist*, 4, 7 (1955) 154–70.

9. ——, 'O ulozi komunista u izgardnji našeg drusťvenog i državnog sistema' [The Role of the Communists in the Development of our Social System], ibid., 481–511.

10. ——, '*Problemi naše socialistioke izgradnje* [Problems of Our Socialist Development], Vol. 2 (Belgrade 1954).

11. O. Lange and F. M. Taylor, *On the Economic Theory of Socialism* (Minneapolis, 1938).

12. A. P. Lerner, *The Economics of Control* (New York, 1946).

13. DJ. Miljević *et al.*, *Razvoj privrednog sistema FNRJ* [The Development of Yugoslavia's Economic System] (Belgrade 1954).

14. D. Misić, 'Ekonomska zastarelost' [Economic Obsolescence], *Ekonomska politika*, 2 (1953) 87–9.

15. L. von Mises, 'Die Wirtschaftsrechnung im sozialen Gemeinwesen', *Archiv f. Sozialwissenschaft*, 47 (1920); English translation in reference 6.

16. J. Sirotković, *Novi privredni sistem FNRJ* [Yugoslavia's New Economic System] (Zagreb, 1954).

17 *Sluzbeni list FNRJ* [Official Gazette of Yugoslavia], Belgrade, 1945.

18. R. Uvalic, 'The Management of Undertakings by the Workers in Yugoslavia' (tr. from Serbo-Croatian), *Internat. Lab. Rev.* 69 (1954) 235–54.

19. B. Ward, 'Workers' Management in Yugoslavia', *Jour. Pol. Econ.*, 65 (Oct 1957) 373–86.

2 Participation and Income Distribution

I. F. Pearce

Rarely has the quarrel over the distribution of income reached such heights of virulence, absorbed so much time and energy of ordinary persons or so dominated the mass communication media as at the present time in the United Kingdom. It is surprising therefore that there has been so little informed comment on at least two errors of logic which underlie almost all the claims and counter-claims put out by sectional interests and which if they were understood would of necessity transform the whole direction of the argument. Scarcely ever is it recognised that:

(i) Whatever kind of system – socialist, communist, capitalist or lilliputian – we care to choose, money and prices will continue to exist and the implied 'natural' income distribution under each and every one would be the same.

(ii) Even if some 'just' distribution of income could be agreed (which it could not) this would not match the 'natural' distribution and would accordingly be impossible to implement in the long run without full-scale direction of labour including circulation by some central authority to individuals of hour-to-hour instructions on how to act, reaching down to the minutest details of economic life.

The first of these errors leads to demands for 'revolution' to 'change the system' to some always unspecified new order defined only by whatever '-ism' is currently fashionable. The second error generates demands for 'fair' treatment in the matter of wages when no one has any notion of what 'fair' is or how justice should be implemented. The result is inflation and in the end repression or chaos.

Consider the current demand for worker participation in industry. It is often said that 'capitalism' is the most potent cause of the maldistribution of income since under capitalism production is designed to maximise the reward of capital rather than the rewards of workers, who 'create the real wealth of the nation'. Worker participation, therefore, would ensure that the interests of labour would be protected. Let us then ask the question what would be the natural distribution of income if the roles of capital and labour were reversed. Suppose that all necessary money capital could be borrowed at a fixed market rate of interest reflecting the competing demands of 'co-operative' industries in the face of scarce resources, and that the objective of each co-operative is to maximise the money reward of its own workforce. Would the material welfare of workers be improved? How would the distribution of income be affected?

We first present the problem in the most general way. There are n consumer goods each produced by a 'collective' employing some of m classes of factors of production – capital, engineers, unskilled labour, etc. Suppose that one class of factor is in control (say the ith). By the ith factor 'in control' we mean that the class i factor organises the collective so as to maximise its own rate of reward, all other classes of factor being rented at agreed market prices. This covers both the case where labour is in charge, renting capital from some government agency, and where shareholders are in charge, renting labour at a wage. We shall see (surprisingly) that it also covers the more embarrassing case where *both* skilled and *unskilled* labour are jointly in charge and have to face the difficult problem of deciding how the rewards of labour should be shared between the two classes; for it turns out that what is best for one factor is best for all (see pp. 30–1).

Whatever the system and whoever is in charge certain facts of nature have to be acknowledged. We set out these constraints on behaviour in the form of equations, commenting upon each in turn. The number of equations is entered just before the Roman numeral identifying the class of equations.

n of (i) $\quad S_i = S_i(A_{il} \ldots \ldots A_{im})$

These are production functions imposed by the laws of physics. Production of the ith commodity S_i is determined by the most efficient use of inputs of factors. A_{ij} is the quantity of the jth factor used in the production S_i of i.

n of (ii) $\quad q_i = q_i(S_1 \ldots \ldots S_n, Y)$

These are market clearing functions expressing the preferences of consumers. Y is the total money expenditure of consumers assumed to be given. q_i is the price of the ith commodity which will just clear the market when amounts $S_1 \ldots S_n$ are supplied. No change of system can alter the market clearing functions.

m of (iii) $\sum_i A_{ij} = A_j$

These equations express the fact that the total usage of the jth factor should, for full employment, exactly equal the total A_j available. We could alternatively have written

$\sum_i A_{ij} = \phi(p_1 \ldots p_m)$ to indicate that the total supply of factors might depend upon the wage structure, but the simpler constraint will illustrate the point. The fact that factor supplies are limited cannot be escaped even after the development of the 'new society'.

We come now to the rules of behaviour which the system imposes. First we have:

n of (iv) $\quad p_{ji} = \dfrac{q_j S_j - \sum\limits_{k \neq i} A_{jk} p_k}{A_{ji}}$

This merely says that the controlling factor i which has formed itself into the jth collective will share equally the difference between revenue

($q_j s_j$) and the cost $\sum\limits_{k \neq i} A_{jk} p_k$ of the non-controlling factors which it rents. p_{ji} is of course the rate of reward for each member of the class of controlling factors organising the jth collective.

$(n \times m)$ of (v) $\quad q_j \dfrac{\partial S_j}{\partial A_{jk}} = \lambda_j p_k.$

or

These equations have to do with the quantity of each factor we should expect the

$$q_j \frac{\partial S_j}{\partial A_{ji}} = \lambda_j p_{ji}$$

j^{th} collective to rent and/or the numbers who should be allowed to join the collective. By definition of the behaviour of the collective, p_{ji} is to be maximised. It follows that, *whatever the chosen level of production, $\bar{S}_j$ of j, p_{ji}* must be maximised subject to the constraint $S_j - \bar{S}_j = 0$. It is impossible that any $\bar{S}_j$ could be the final chosen level of output unless the maximising condition is satisfied. It follows that equations (v) would have to hold whatever the social system. Alternatively, we might note that the equations (v) would have to hold if the cost of any given output $\bar{S}_j$ were to be minimised i.e. for $\sum_{k \neq i} A_{jk} p_k + p_{ji} A_{ji}$ to be minimised. Obviously, it would be absurd for any collective to produce a given output at more than minimum cost since it could raise everyone's reward by changing the technique of production, keeping total production constant.

$(n-1)$ of (vi) $p_{ki} = p_{ji}$

for all k, j

Provided collectives could be formed at will with any number of participants it is clearly impossible for the rewards of individual controlling units to differ. If they differ it would be in the interests of some group of controlling factors to form a new co-operative to compete with those that have proved themselves the more successful. New collectives would copy the behaviour of those earning the greater reward. Only by creating monopolies or by introducing laws to restrict the right to certain kinds of behaviour would it be possible to hold $p_{ki} \neq p_{ji}$ in the long run.

Now add equations and unknowns. We have

Equations	*Unknowns*
n of (i)	n of q_i
n of (ii)	n of S_i
m of (iii)	$(m-1)$ of p_k $(k \neq i)$
n of (iv)	n of λ_j
$(n \times m)$ of (v)	$(n \times m)$ of A_{ij}
$(n-1)$ of (vi)	n of p_{ji}

Evidently all unknowns are determined. Provided all six rules of nature or behaviour are satisfied one and only one set of factor prices is possible. The distribution of income between various classes of labour and between labour and capital is uniquely determined, as we say, 'by the laws of supply and demand'. Any departure from the given distribution necessarily implies a departure from one or more of the six rules. But the six rules must apply to any system.

Under capitalism shareholders (or management) play the part of factor *i*. With collectives some class of labour is in control. Or possibly it may be agreed that all workers should participate. But if this is the case agreement on the share to go to each class of worker could be quickly reached, for wage rates are the same even if one or other factor gives up its 'control' rights. The numbers employed in each collective are exactly those which would be employed if each class of factor in turn as asked to choose that which is most satisfactory to itself. The payment to each factor is exactly what it would get if it was invited to ignore the rights of all other factors and do the best it could for itself. All factors in the same class are paid the same reward by condition (vi). Given this condition the maximising equations under (v) are exactly symmetric for every factor. Allowing a factor to be 'exploited' by some controlling factor leads to exactly the same result as would be the case if the 'exploited' factor were in turn allowed to do the exploiting. The activities of the controlling factor actually maximise the rewards available to all other factors. Suppose in fact that the system provided for an 'agreed' share-out of revenue within the collective, and suppose some different share-out than that determined by equations (i) – (vi) was decided upon. Since equations (v) would not then hold it would appear to each collective that its costs for a given output were not minimised. It would seem that further profits could be earned by changing the technique of production, i.e. the proportions in which each class of factor was employed within the collective. But if this was attempted unemployment would ensue (breakdown of equation (vi)) or some factors would offer their services voluntarily (to avoid unemployment) at a lower reward. These adjustments would cease only when the distribution came to be exactly that consistent with the facts of life as expressed in the equations.

It is worth noting that the only way in which a different pattern of wage and interest distribution could be attained consistently with equations (i) – (vi) would be by altering the overall supply of factor A_j. If engineers are paid too much the supply of engineers will be increased. If on the other hand we require that the choice of a profession should be a matter for the individual rather than the state, and if we suppose that each individual is free to choose his profession in accordance with the observed pattern of rewards $p_1 \ldots p_m$, then instead of equations (iii) we should have to write $\sum_i A_{ij} = A_j (p_1 \ldots p_m)$. But this would make no difference whatever to the equation counting. We should now have to say that conditions governing the supply of factors are just as much a fact of life as any of the other rules. Each factor would be receiving the reward it chose to receive when the free decision to enter the given profession was made subject only to the same constraints (facts of life) as apply to all other citizens. Any case alleging maldistribution of income would then have to be made on the basis of a claim that choice of profession could not be freely made: the individual lacked inborn talent or the opportunity to acquire a suitable education. Alternatively, it might be argued that an individual would have entered a different profession were it not for some mistake made earlier in his career. This would form the basis of a case for the provision of adult educational opportunities. What becomes clear is that changing the system of industrial organisation will not, of itself, change the distribution of income. Greater equality of opportunity is likely to have more effect whatever the political system. Equality of income should not be mistaken for equality of opportunity. Equal opportunity could lead and probably would lead to very great inequality of income since many individuals would be prepared (indeed would insist upon) trading income for leisure or for a more relaxed way of life.

INCOME FROM CAPITAL

The foregoing section proves that, provided capital is scarce (which it is) and provided scarce capital is rationed by a price system, price will be the same under socialism or capitalism or any other political regime that anyone might care to invent, other than pure planning without prices. However, it could be argued that if the ownership of capital were removed from persons and transferred to government by some political act then this would at the same time transfer the income from capital from a few wealthy persons to the government, so that all might share.

The first point to note about this is that the same argument might apply to the reward for labour. Any government could, by a political act, tax away all the revenue from labour so that it might be shared by all. Workers would then become slaves of the government. Neither of these acts at all affects equations (i) – (vi). The reward received by the factors are the same under all systems. The only thing which is different is ownership of the factors. The redistribution of income achieved would be due to the transfer of ownership and not to any change in industrial organisation by (say) worker participation.

Note also another difference. Suppose that if was considered proper to transfer to government all ownership of capital and hence income from it. What would then happen in a world of collectives? Individuals would save some part of their income. This would now afford the opportunity for collectives to improve the rewards to their members by borrowing new capital required from individuals rather than government until the free market rate of interest was competed up to the government rate. The act of expropriation of capital would then have to be repeated at intervals to the natural and eventual discouragement of savers. Suppose with this in mind the government chose to prevent all saving either by making saving illegal or by discouragement through periodical expropriations. It would then be necessary for the government to save by taxation or by raising the price charged to collectives for capital, which can be interpreted as an indirect form of taxation. To put the matter in terms of equations (i) – (vi) it would be the case that the failure by individuals to save would reduce the amount of scarce capital available (equation (iii)) and force up the price accordingly. This would be an act of interference in the market by government which would have the effect of reducing saving by some individuals, so eliminating their reward for that service, substituting in place of private saving an equal measure of forced saving on the community as a whole. The community as a whole would receive the income from the forced saving indirectly through an increase in government revenue. This is obviously socially inefficient. People who wish to save, given the reward, are prevented from doing so. People who do not wish to save are forced to do so by government decree. This is exactly equivalent to an order to (say) a coalminer, who chooses to work at the coal-face for high pay, to work some time on the surface, combined with an order to the surface worker to work some time at the coal-face, the whole exercise being designed to equalise the incomes of the two individuals. Interference of this kind could be justified only if it could be shown that lack of opportunity rather than choice determines professions.

Of course, it could be argued that ownership of capital is due more to inheritance than to personal saving; but if this is so, and it is less so at the present time than many people believe, then this is an argument for an inheritance tax rather than a new and revolutionary 'system'.

WINDFALL PROFITS

Equations (i)–(vi) do exhibit one asymmetric feature worthy of note. These equations define a stationary state rather than a truism. There need not always be full employment, market prices need not always be that which just equates supply and demand, costs are not always minimised when technical change is taking place. It could be argued that it matters a great deal which factor is the controlling factor since by equation (iv) the controlling factor receives all 'windfall' profits. Windfall profits are those which sometimes accrue in out-of-equilibrium situations. If demand changes, the first co-operative to respond will earn in the short run a profit over and above the norm. Could it not be the case that worker participation would offer a great advantage over 'capitalism' because of the opportunity it affords to share the windfall gains? In this connection it should be pointed out that we have no evidence to show that windfall gains are earned any more frequently than windfall losses are suffered. It may well be that any gain to be made by choosing the role of controlling factor is more than offset by the uncertainty of associated reward. At any rate this would seem to be a view implicitly expressed by many trade unionists at the present time.

RETURNS TO SCALE

In setting out equations (i)–(vi) no mention was made of the structure of markets. The argument does not rest upon any assumption of 'perfect competition' in the technical meaning of the expression. Note especially the implications of equations (iv) and (v). Multiplying both sides of (v) by A_{jk} and summing we have:

$$\sum_{k \neq i} q_j \frac{\partial S_j}{\partial A_{jk}} A_{jk} + q_j \frac{\partial S_j}{\partial A_{ji}} A_{ji} = \lambda_j \left(\sum p_k A_{jk} + p_{ji} A_{ji} \right) = \lambda_j q_j S_j$$

or using (vi) $\sum_k \frac{\partial S}{\partial A_{jk}} A_{jk} = \lambda_j S_j$

In other words λ_j is a measure of returns to scale. Let us suppose that, for any collective j, constant returns to scale are observed when all equations (i)–(vi) are satisfied. It would then be true (from (v)) that

$$q_j \frac{\partial S_j}{\partial A_{jk}} = p_k$$

and

$$q_j \frac{\partial S_j}{\partial A_{ji}} = p_{ji}$$

This implies that the collective j is choosing a scale of output S_j which maximises the rate of return to the controlling factor as well as the most advantageous technique of production for the given level of output. It is clear then that as long as rules (i)–(vi) generate an equilibrium which leaves each collective in position showing constant returns to scale locally there will be no incentive to change the scale of operation or to introduce a new collective. Some comment is necessary however in the case where constant returns to scale are not observed.

We may at once eliminate all possibilities of diminishing returns to scale (i.e. $\lambda_j < 1$), for in such a case the collective might straightaway increase the wage rate of the controlling factor by reducing their numbers. Only if the collective membership is legally fixed does it make sense to produce in the area of decreasing returns and even then only if there exists some legal impediment to prevent competition by a newly-formed collective producing a similar product.

In the case of increasing returns let us suppose that the number of collectives in existence is fixed and equations (i)–(vi) hold. If the jth collective now observes the possibility of reducing cost by increased output ($\lambda_j > 1$) then it may wish to do this, provided only it thinks that the price q_j of the product will not be correspondingly reduced by the increased sales. Suppose it does increase production. In this case it may or may not earn a greater wage for the controlling factor. If it does not it will return to the *status quo*. If it does competitors will copy the more successful behaviour bringing down the price q_j until the excess earnings are competed away. What equations (i)–(vi) tell us is that as long as the number of collectives (equations) remain the same the process described is bound to end up in the same position of equilibrium from which it started, namely the position where equations (i)–(vi) are satisfied for all collectives.

Some economists might wish to describe this process as 'discovering the demand curve for the product'. Collectives would find by experience that it is impossible to sell at a price inside a certain cost curve and that it is possible to sell only at one price which is actually on that cost curve (i.e. at that point where equations (i)–(iv) are satisfied everywhere). If this is interpreted to mean that a demand curve exists for the product tangent to the cost curve at that equilibrium point then λ_j (equation (v)) will measure the parameter $\dfrac{E}{E+1}$ where E is the elasticity of demand for the product. Equations (v) then are equivalent to the statement that marginal cost equals marginal revenue, which is the economist's notion of the optimum scale of production.

The present writer does not favour this interpretation, however, since it is both confusing and unnecessary. Equations (i)–(vi) identify the correct equilibrium without recourse to any concept of demand other than the market clearing functions (ii). The argument is included here only to make it clear to the reader that the symmetry of equations (i)–(vi) holds even in the case where market prices are not taken by collectives to be constants unaffected by their output strategy provided only there is sufficient 'monopolistic' competition to ensure that homogeneous factors receive similar rewards (equations (vi)).

Of course, when increasing returns are present there may be an incentive for collectives to amalgamate. But the equations show that this incentive in no way depends upon choice of controlling factor. However much 'participation' is encouraged, the final solution is bound to be the same as the standard result for the 'capitalist' system even under the usual monopolistic competition assumptions. Under any political system there is a natural pattern of income distribution which is the same for all political systems and which can be interfered with only by some carefully thought-out system of taxation or by activity designed to alter the supply of the various classes of labour.

The belief that a change in 'the system' will solve our economic problems is a myth. Even if it were true that great profits are made out of risks taken in 'out-of-equilibrium' situations, is it to be supposed that there exists some possible institutional change which would induce different and perhaps more worthy persons to bear risk and receive reward for it? It seems hardly likely. As soon as the new system came to be understood the same individuals would come forward to bear the same burden for the same reasons. And from their activity, all would gain.

Plus ça change – plus c'est le même chose.

3 Some Effects of Worker Participation and the Distribution of Income

C. J. Hawkins

INTRODUCTION

Professor Pearce asserts that, provided money and prices continue to exist, then the implied 'natural' income distribution will be the same whether capitalists or workers run the system. Capitalism, he argues, does not exploit labour; quite the contrary, in fact, since in his model capitalism is shown to maximise wages. No amount of socialism, Marxism or workers' participation could increase wages since these are already and always will be under capitalism, at a maximum. In short, worker control is shown to yield exactly the same income distribution as control by capitalists.

This paper analyses the conditions necessary for Pearce's conclusions to hold, argues that they are not met with in reality, in our economy at least, and goes on to show that, using an alternative approach, we can establish at least *a priori* grounds for believing that worker participation *could* alter the distribution of income and might even bring about an increase in welfare in the sense that everybody could be made better off.

ANALYSIS OF THE PEARCE MODEL

1. Pearce asserts that production functions are 'imposed by the laws of physics'. This is the standard neo-classical assumption. Unfortunately, it is surely one of the most unrealistic assumptions ever made by neo-classical economists. Production functions are in reality imposed by the laws of humanity not of physics. People are not molecules, behaving in a constant, consistent, mechanical fashion, always the same, invariably

yielding an identical response to a given set of stimuli. People are a composite of likes, dislikes, emotions, urges, morals and much more. They need motivating to give of their best. Their best varies from day to day, from place to place, from factory to factory. No two human inputs are identical. One hundred men under one manager will produce a different output from the same men under a different manager. Man can vary the quality and quantity of his output. His output almost never achieves the maximum of which he is capable; the difference between this and what he actually achieves has been called 'X-inefficiency' Liebenstein [1966].

If it is agreed that 'X-inefficiency' exists then production functions are not determined only by the laws of physics. There is no unique relationship between inputs and outputs. This problem is returned to in the next section.

2. It is very possible that if the system were run by workers for workers, the men on the shop floor might produce far more from given resources than they do under a system which they *may* see as being run by capitalists, for capitalists. We cannot therefore assume as the Pearce model does, that total incomes are given (i.e. that $Y = \bar{Y}$) since the sum total of incomes must equal the sum total value of outputs, which can vary with human effort and motivation. It is at least possible that improved motivation via worker participation could lead to higher output and therefore higher wages.

3. Firms are assumed to cost-minimise and to maximise revenue minus cost. For them to succeed perfectly in doing this, which is necessary for the Pearce equilibrium to be reached and his conclusions to hold, we need to assume:

(*a*) that they want to;

(*b*) that they know how to;

(*c*) that they have perfect knowledge of all relevant information.

There is an extensive literature which casts doubt on all three of these assumptions (see Hawkins [1973] for a summary and bibliography). For example, managers may choose not to minimise cost but instead to have large expense accounts and company cars. Equally, they may choose to maximise revenue or output or sales and would not then achieve the Pearce equilibrium which maximises profits and wages. There is, too, a growing body of thought that firms may not aim to maximise anything but may instead aim for satisfactory levels of important variables. Many motives are possible. This is especially so now that ownership and control are divorced in most industrial enterprises: the 'capitalist' has been replaced by shareholders who own, and managers who manage. Managers do not receive the profits and so may well choose to maximise other things – such as their own self-interest, which is not necessarily synonymous with profit.

Equally if worker control is allowed, it is necessary for the three assumptions above to apply to them, which seems open to even more doubt. For example, the particular workers who are put in control and asked to maximise total wages for the rest may well find conflicts with their own personal gain. They, like managers, might enjoy excessive expense accounts and empire-building, might pay themselves too high a wage, take too much time off and make unnecessary private telephone calls. Workers in control of one firm might resist a merger that would create redundancies even if by moving elsewhere those who lost their jobs could stay in work and even if total wages would benefit. Human beings, whether we like it or not, often put themselves first, their group second and all mankind third.

Whoever runs the system, the number of permutations of inputs that must be worked out in order to optimise is vast, and few if any managers are even aware of the techniques necessary to solve the problems involved. And the amount of information needed on costs, on demand, on the effects of advertising and so on is so enormous that the idea that managers or workers could have adequate data to achieve the Pearce equilibrium is surely beyond theoretical or practical belief. Nor is information about the present all that is needed. To take correct decisions the decision-maker must have the power of predicting future values of relevant variables which not even the most confident clairvoyant would claim.

Admittedly, Pearce argues that firms could not possibly know their demand curve – a view that has long been held by many industrial economists, though for somewhat different reasons. Pearce does, however, assume that firms accurately know the minimum cost of producing all feasible levels of output. Factor prices are taken as given. But it is difficult to see why the arguments applied to demand should not equally apply to costs of production. Every move a firm makes must affect factor prices. And actions and reactions of all other firms must do so as well. None of us has the power to predict, with perfect accuracy, the behaviour of each and every decision-making unit in the economy – let alone the exact effect that their decisions will have on the price of all factors of production. Lacking this ability and living as we do in a highly complex world where the movements of every firm affect the conditions facing every other, it would be incorrect and contrary to any firm's actual experience for it to assume factor prices are given and immutable. Under these conditions it seems implausible that firms could ever accurately know their cost curves, or perfectly succeed in minimising cost, in maximising profit (or anything else) except by coincidence.

4. Pearce asserts that if rewards to controlling groups differed, new groups would form and compete away any differences that existed. This clearly requires that there be free entry into all industries, no patents, nor any other barriers to entry. There is an extensive literature establishing the widespread existence of barriers to entry in practice (see Hawkins

[1973] for further references). As a result we cannot assume that profits would everywhere be equal and would be eroded down to the 'normal' rate of profit when capitalists run the system. Nor can we, without this assumption, show from the model as currently specified that it will make no difference whether capitalists or workers run the system. Far from it, since whichever side runs the system will make sure that it gets the surplus profits made possible by the barriers to free entry into some industries. With barriers to entry these supernormal profits may persist for very long periods if not for ever.

5. It is surely not enough to say, as Pearce does, that if economies of scale exist 'competitors will copy the more successful behaviour . . . until the excess earnings are competed away'. This completely ignores the fact that the economies of scale may themselves act as a barrier or deterrent to entry; entry at a level of output which would make production at a competitive cost possible might create excess demand and drive price below production costs. So the new entrant does not enter and the existing firms can continue to make supernormal profits forever. For example, see the model developed by Modigliani [1964], and for a summary of the extensive literature on this problem see Hawkins [1973]. Any supernormal profits earned when barriers to entry existed could accrue to capitalists or to workers, depending on which of them ran the system.

6. In industries where economies of scale are not big enough to deter entry, capitalism achieves the well-known tangency solution as is seen in the Pearce model. It is perhaps possible that socialism or some form of government intervention could improve this solution by reducing the number of firms so that those who remain can produce at minimum average cost. Worker participation might not achieve this, but government intervention might, although individual capitalists maximising their own returns have no incentive and no means of solving this problem. It is not perhaps fair to say socialism could not affect the distribution of income. It could nationalise this industry, reduce the number of firms and make all produce at minimum long run average cost.

7. Even if none of the objections above held, the Pearce model is still only one for static equilibrium. It says that if we wait long enough for the capitalist system to reach equilibrium, wages will be maximised. While it is out of equilibrium, there is no evidence at all that they will. And since we live in a world of continual change, of new ideas, new booms and new slumps, we are out of equilibrium most of the time. It is not enough, in my view, to say we do not know whether, when the system is out of equilibrium, profits are greater than losses. All standard economic analysis suggests widespread supernormal profits out of equilibrium while waiting for new firms (or new collectives) to start production and erode these profits away. We have lived in a world of oligopoly and

monopoly for decades if not generations. ICI and General Motors have existed for a very long time now. Losses are mainly due to errors of judgement caused by firms not having the perfect information assumed by the Pearce model. Equilibrium could not be reached without it. With such information firms would, at least in general, make excess profits while out of equilibrium. Kodak, General Motors and others have made high rates of return for long periods. These would accrue to workers if they ran the system and to capitalists if they did.

8. Even if one could show that capitalism maximised wages in a real-world situation, this would not, as I see it, be the same as saying that worker control would make no difference. On the assumptions of the model capitalists must select 'the best man for the job' to minimise costs. Workers have not been selected to manage and so must, it follows in this model, be less good at managing. As a result worker control should reduce incomes in the model as specified.

9. Pearce asserts that his 'six rules of nature or behaviour . . . must apply to any system'. But in what sense are they *rules* of nature or behaviour? Aren't they merely assumptions convenient to the model? And why must they apply to any system? Why could we not maximise output subject to a profit constraint (as many communist countries do)? Or give some goods away free and ration them (as we do with higher education in Britain, and with health and roads)?

10. Changing the rules may infringe efficiency as valued at market prices. But is efficiency the supreme God? Must we sell what people want to buy even if it is bad for them? Do market prices really correctly value the optimum use of resources or don't we need to look at social costs and benefits?

11. We are told that distributions of income which are not 'Pearce Natural' 'would be impossible to implement in the long run without full-scale direction of labour'. Some further proof would be interesting since our economy and many others do manage to soldier on without direction of labour yet having numerous distortions from the assumptions needed for the model's equilibrium distribution. Or is direction of labour only needed to achieve efficiency as defined by the model? In this case we might prefer other approaches such as more equality and less efficiency.

12. Personally I do not see why we should want to maximise either wages or profit. To do either has heavy costs and involves frequent redundancies, bankruptcies and mergers. We might prefer fewer people to be forced to move out of the Scottish Highlands. And some of us may feel maximising money or happiness is a rather hedonistic and distasteful approach to life.

THE PEARCE MODEL: SUMMARY AND CONCLUSIONS

1. None of the foregoing is intended to deny the utmost importance of some of the central conclusions of the Pearce model. The model shows that if society wants to minimise costs, and can perfectly succeed in doing so and in being efficient in all the ways specified, and if society will accept the unequal distribution of incomes that will result, then – on certain specified assumptions – control by capitalists will maximise wages and will give the same distribution of incomes as would control by workers.

2. The fact that many of the assumptions are of questionable real-world validity is not too important if, instead of using the model to draw conclusions about the world as it exists, we instead use it as one guide to the kind of ideal world for which those who want to maximise wages should strive. It is in this sense that the model is seen here to be important.

3. But even as a description of one kind of ideal world the model suffers from the following:

(*a*) it relates only to long-run static equilibrium. En route to equilibrium worker control might raise wages since the excess profits, which may then be a normal feature of the system, could be distributed amongst workers, instead of accruing to capitalists as they would under a capitalist system.

(*b*) Even in long-run equilibrium worker control could increase wages if any industries existed in which barriers to entry had prevented profits from being eroded down to 'normal'.

(*c*) Workers would need to be totally convinced (perhaps wrongly in view of (*a*) and (*b*) above) that capitalism in this ideal world did in fact maximise wages. This is necessary so that 'X-inefficiency' would be no greater amongst workers when capitalists were in charge than it would be if they were in charge themselves. The probable widespread existence of 'X-inefficiency', with the possibility that its extent may vary depending on who runs the system, is important because it destroys the idea of a unique relationship between inputs and output, the idea of a single production function for each product – ideas which are specifically made central to the Pearce model.

4. It is argued that the arguments used to question the existence of a known demand curve could be applied equally well to the existence of known cost curves.

5. The criticisms, above, apply not just to the model as a description of an ideal world, but also to its use for drawing conclusions about reality. Two additional real-world problems are:

(*a*) firms lack the information needed to minimise cost, maximise profit, and in general to achieve the static equilibrium specified.

(*b*) managers – who now largely run the present 'capitalist' system – may not even be trying to minimise and maximise in the ways specified.

(*c*) equally, it is argued that the Pearce model takes only one of many possible motivations for workers' leaders when it analyses the effect of their being in control.

In the following section possible gains and losses of worker participation or control are outlined in more detail, and an alternative to the static equilibrium approach is suggested for evaluating them.

POSSIBLE GAINS AND LOSSES FROM WORKER PARTICIPATION

1. One possible loss from worker participation or complete worker control might be that workers might not choose to behave in such a way as to maximise total wages. They might instead try to maximise wages for the present number of employees in their firm, or to do this but subject to the constraint that no one loses their job. Closed shops might be established to preclude free entry into an industry leading to higher prices and lower output than a more competitive system would yield. Clearly excess 'profits' could then result—perhaps taken in the form of higher than necessary wages. Distortions somewhat like those of monopoly capitalism could equally well occur under a system of worker control. There would be – potentially at least – losses of output and welfare for society as a whole, resulting from some of the many possible policies which workers in control could choose to pursue.

2. A second major loss could result from the fact that participation might be costly. For example, the cost of training worker representatives in management techniques, the cost of giving more information to the shop floor, the cost of changing from our present system to a new one, and so on.

3. A third example of the kind of losses that might result from worker participation or worker control is that workers might be less good at managing than managers are. Wrong decisions might be taken and companies might in general be run less well. Electing one or two worker directors, or having workers' representatives on a supervisory board (as is often done in Germany) would seem to be one way of minimising this particular problem, at least as a first approach.

4. The major potential gain from worker participation is that it might reduce the extent to which alienation of the workforce can lead to disruption of the system. If workers believed that capitalism maximised

wages there would presumably be no trade unions—or at any rate no unions involved in wage bargaining. There does seem to be a widely-held view in Britain, and elsewhere, that the main result of shop-floor effort will only be an increase in profits. As a result, 'X-inefficiency' (the gap between the quantity and quality of output which a man produces and that which he is humanly capable of) is almost certainly very large.

The case for worker participation, or for full worker control, is that employees would more fully believe that their efforts would affect their rewards, would accept the system as fair (or fairer) and as a result would put in much more effort –thereby reducing 'X-inefficiency'.
5. This implies more output from a given quantity of inputs in each firm, and therefore higher aggregate output and higher aggregate incomes. Just who would benefit from the change of system would clearly depend on the distribution of incomes and taxation that was chosen, but if more output was produced clearly some distribution would exist which could make all better off. Firms' costs of production would be lowered and society's production possibility frontier would be pushed outwards nearer to its theoretical maximum.

The original concept of 'X-inefficiency' is not specifically related to alienation. It exists because labour can vary both the quality and quantity of its output. (Traditionally economists would argue that the wage should vary to reflect variations in different men's output, so perhaps one should add that complete supervision all the time is neither possible nor economic. Perfect knowledge of everyone's marginal product is not possible. And in addition institutional factors, such as unions, often make it necessary to pay everyone the same wage in a given class of occupation. Having employed someone, it is often impossible, or expensive, to fire them even if they are not thought to have a marginal revenue product as great as their wage.)

If workers believe that extra effort from them will merely increase profits, and if they think only capitalists will benefit from the profits, and if they get no pleasure from increasing the welfare of capitalists, then they have no incentive to expend more effort than the minimum they can get away with, or the least amount they think is fair for the pay they get – whichever is the higher of these two. But if by introducing a measure of worker participation (as, say, Germany has done) and if as a result people felt that more effort from them meant either

    (*a*) higher wages for them
or (*b*) higher wages for their workmates
or (*c*) higher living standards for society as a whole
or (*d*) a combination of some or all of the above

then in all probability people would work harder or better or both. They might do so if they cared only for their own gains (if they believed (*a*) above) – up to the point where the marginal utility of their extra wages equalled the marginal disutility of the extra effort needed to generate the wages. More socially minded people could, in addition, attach utility to higher wages for their workmates and for society as a whole – (*b*) and (*c*) above – and could increase effort to the point where the marginal utility to them of all these gains equalled the marginal disutility of their extra effort.

In this way – although we might not create a society in which all gave maximum effort – at least we might create one in which most wanted to do a good deal more than the minimum that it was possible to get away with.

An additional major gain from worker participation might be an increase in investment on a long-run basis. It is frequently argued that many firms, especially the large multinationals, are investing less and less in countries noted for labour disputes, failing to meet delivery schedules, shoddy workmanship and the like – all fairly plausible results of an alienated workforce. Worker participation if it improved motivation to work, increased industrial harmony, and reduced production costs by enabling us to get more output from a given quantity of inputs – worker participation might then lead to a significant increase in investment both in the short and the long run. And this could lead to an increase in the economy's long-run growth rate.

7. Given the continually changing nature of the world economy, and of the potential gains and losses from worker participation (which might increase – or decrease – over time) it may not be particularly useful to use the static equilibrium approach for assessing whether or not a particular policy is worth while. In a dynamic world of continual change, perhaps it would be more useful to try to evaluate gains and losses year by year over whatever time-horizon is thought reasonable. Net benefits – or losses – in each year could then be discounted back to the present day at whatever discount rate is thought appropriate for the society in question. The cost/benefit approach is usually used for microeconomic decisions. In this case one would be applying it to assess changes in the whole economy – a mammoth task.

8. The problems of estimation are horrific. My personal view is that we are in no position to make realistic detailed estimates at present. We can compare efficiency levels in, say, British plants with levels in similar plants elsewhere. But we do not know to what extent participation would help to equate the two – or what precise effects moves in the right direction would have on investment.

We can, as always in this kind of situation, fall back on our own judgement – our best guess at the results of a policy change; or we can let elected politicians use their judgement to decide for us. It might pay to experiment. We could try participation not in all companies, all at once, but in some major, some medium and some minor ones. We could monitor the situation in each, assess the impact of the changes and then, with the extra information gained, make estimates of the effects of implementing participation on a more general basis.

9. Until detailed information is available on the costs and benefits of participation, as outlined above, it is not possible to say whether a policy to promote worker participation in industry would or would not be beneficial. But it is argued here that we cannot *theoretically* rule out the possibility that participation may pay. The costs may be high but so too are the potential gains both in higher output and in higher investment.

10. The gains and losses so far outlined in this section relate to society as a whole. Any net gains could be used to improve wages or to improve profits or to improve both. As already shown in the analysis of the Pearce model, worker participation or control could also lead to higher wages even if it did not lead to increases in output and/or investment. It could do so by reallocating to labour any super-normal profits made by firms when out of equilibrium and the super-normal profits made both in and out of equilibrium by firms which were protected from free competition by barriers to entry.

REFERENCES

Hawkins, C. J. [1973], *Theory of the Firm* (Macmillan).
Liebenstein, H. [1966], 'Allocative Efficiency Versus X-Efficiency' *American Economic Review*, 56.
Modigliani, F. [1958], 'New Developments on the Oligopoly Front', *Journal of Political Economy*, 66.

4 Participation and the Working of the Price Mechanism in a Market Economy

Joachim Gäbler

The idea of worker participation in economic decisions on various levels is getting more and more popular or – among its opponents – unpopular in an increasing number of West European countries. It is, therefore, a little surprising that so much of the discussion on participation is left by economists to political philosophers and politicians dwelling on the moral beauty or ugliness of the whole idea and treating the possible economic consequences of participation in a most superficial way. Economists should take up the discussion on these consequences of participation seriously. With my paper I should like to stimulate discussion of the question: Will the general introduction of a high degree of workers' participation in the decisions of industrial enterprises improve or impair the performance of our market economy or eventually be incompatible with a sufficiently working market economy?

I feel that as yet the following questions on the importance of participation for the working of market mechanisms are only unsatisfactorily answered:

1. What interests will co-determining employees have and how will they change the objective functions of co-determined enterprises?
2. How will changed objective functions of co-determined firms influence their market behaviour?
3. What consequences will this changed market behaviour have for the performance of the whole market economy from the point of view of important objectives of economic policy?
4. How must economic policy change under conditions of general co-determination in order to achieve its aims?

I think it is quite obvious that for methodological reasons economists are reluctant to speculate on this kind of question. We feel we are walking on relatively safe ground as long as we are asked to develop theories on existing economic systems which can be tested empirically or theories on the presumable effects of marginal and quantitative changes within a qualitatively constant socio-economic structure; but we feel on wobbly ground as soon as we are asked to speculate on people's behaviour in an unknown future society which differs from the present economic system fundamentally. Could not the general introduction of participation mean such a fundamental social change that economists cannot justify any prediction on the results of a participatory economy?

To this methodological difficulty must be added that of the vagueness of the notion of 'participation'. There are many forms and degrees of worker participation on various levels which are possible and under discussion, and each model of participation is likely to work differently in countries with different social and political 'climates'. It is, therefore, obvious that any 'general' theory of a participatory economy would be nonsense. Only theories of well-specified forms of participation for economies under similar social conditions can be useful.

In my paper I shall try to avoid the pitfalls of purely utopian speculations on some vague participatory fool's paradise by concentrating on that model of participation on the company level which is demanded by the trade unions and the Social Democrats in West Germany: the model of 'parity' participation of employees in the supervisory boards of companies, which would give equal voting rights to the representatives of capital-owners and employees on the board. As to the behaviour to be expected under such a system of participation I shall make the hypothesis that it will be similar to that which can be observed under the present system of participation in parts of West German industry and the system of workers' self-administration in Yugoslavia.

THE INTERESTS AND OBJECTIVE FUNCTIONS OF CO-DETERMINED ENTERPRISES.

It may safely be assumed that, whatever the interests of workers may be, their influence on their firm's policy will not be very strong as long as workers have less than 50 per cent of the votes on those boards of a company that actually make important decisions. For West Germany at least we can say that co-determination in those industries in which the employees' representatives have only one-third of the seats on each company's supervisory board (all industries except the coal and steel industries) has hardly damaged the profit interests of capitalists: to the extent that it means an improved flow of information from management to employees and unions, integration of employees' representatives in decision processes may well have improved their understanding of and feeling of responsibility for their companies' difficulties. It may therefore have tempered wage claims in critical situations, reduced the propensity to strike and the level of social tensions generally. Such a mild form of participation, giving responsibility to employees without equal power, may be better suited to capitalists' profit interests in the long run than an unmitigated class struggle in capitalist economies without participation.

This is indicated by the fact that even very conservative German entrepreneurs do not oppose seriously this system while they fiercely fight against the idea of a general introduction of parity participation. Even if the 50 per cent share of workers' representatives in boards separates effective from ineffective co-determination one should distinguish between formal and material parity. If employees take 50 per cent of the seats on some supervisory board that formally directs a company's business policy while actually the company's management or 'technostructure' makes important decisions independently, parity co-determination will in practice be much less impressive than on paper. Thus, in West Germany, limitation of the principle of parity co-determination in the coal and steel industries to the companies' supervisory boards did not decisively diminish the power of the companies' managing committees, in which workers had only a minority representation. Under the British system of companies' boards parity representation might give workers more power than under the German system. On the other hand, even a less than parity share of employees' votes on a board may guarantee a majority for the workers if the state owns at least a part of the capital and the state's representatives on the board are, under political pressure, forced to vote with the workers' representatives. In the same way additional trade union pressure from within the company or from outside will increase the influence of the 'worker directors' beyond their minority position. Certainly the degree of directness of workers' influence will be important for the kind of decisions to be expected. Some form of direct 'grass-roots' democracy in companies may result in decisions in accordance with the real subjective interests of a company's employees while a more indirect form of workers' representation by delegates from a central trade union's 'élite' may filter and modify the workers' immediate demands considerably. In the German discussion on participation all well-known arguments for and against direct or indirect democracy are repeated again and again. While some fear and detest the arrogance of a trade union bureaucracy and of big labour bosses interfering in business affairs from outside the companies others hope that a trade union élite will show more responsibility for the interests and needs of the national economy, that it will be guided by reason more than by emotion, by long-term interests rather than by short-sighted selfishness, and that its business policy will be less erratic (Seidel [1973]). In Germany the embittered haggling of political parties, trade unions and employers' associations over systems of selection of candidates and other organisational details proves that they are well aware of the importance of these institutional regulations for the decisions of co-determined firms.

Even if we discuss well-specified forms of participation we would be naïve to deduce from them a particular behaviour in business affairs without taking into account the whole social background – the social climate of the country which is to introduce participation. Do workers and their organisations accept a participatory economy as a permanent system from which a 'fair deal' between capital and labour interests can be expected? Or do they see participation as a weapon in a continuing class struggle, to be used in order to destroy hated capitalism and to proceed – by revolution or by evolution – from the capitalist swindle to co-determination? In the former case, workers' representatives may use their power in some system of co-determination in order to lubricate the gears of a market economy, in the latter for throwing sand in its gearbox. If, as in West Germany, participation, even the parity participation in the coal and steel industries, has worked quite well, it may be partly due to the special political circumstances of divided post-war Germany in which during the cold war any socialist alternatives to the 'social market economy' were unpopular and unacceptable to a majority of the members of trade unions. Even in the present economic crisis I believe that from the point of view of trade unions' attitude and of the general 'social climate' co-determination in Germany will work less against the principles of market economy than in West and South European countries with strong Marxist parties and trade unions or in Great Britain with non-Marxist but radical and class-conscious unions.

As to the economic interests of co-determining workers a wide spectrum of speculations exist. One extreme assumption is that workers' interests are completely independent of their right to participate in their firm's decision, and that their explicit or implicit present selfish interest in, for example maximisation of their income or safety of employment in the same job and the same plant, will also determine their attitude in co-determined firms. Others reject such a theory of anthropological constants in economic behaviour as naïve. Much of the optimism of Marxists concerning socialism, for example, stems from the optimistic anthropological theory that man, after the abolition of private ownership of productive means and the 'alienation' connected with it, will feel work without material incentives to be an elementary and urgent desire, and social solidarity and brotherly co-operation without special economic rewards will prevail. Although, of course, Marxists deny that mere participation without 'socialisation' of productive means can bring about such a qualitative change of social values and interests. But clearly many protagonists of workers' participation are motivated by the hope that workers, if they get entrepreneurial rights and responsibilities, will feel a new dignity and develop a new moral system unknown to workers who feel their labour treated as just another commodity.

I would not like to ridicule these hopes, but instead of speculating in the dark, I feel, the best we can do now is to analyse the behaviour of employees and their representatives under existing systems of co-determination or self-administration to obtain some hints at presumable behaviour of our workers in a future general system of participation.

The sad history of most workers' co-operatives in capitalist countries in the past is well known: poor market performance due to lack of managerial authority and frequent undecided disputes between the partners of the cooperative, limitation of entry of new partners, withdrawal of capital by members and lack of initiative very often let them founder. I doubt, however, whether much can be learnt from these experiences for problems of contemporary participation. Members of these co-operatives were capital-owners as well as labourers, and in most cases these co-operatives had only a small share in the production of their industry. Experiences from co-operatives in most East European socialist economies are also of very limited value for an analysis of problems of participation in our market economies, because decisions of these co-operatives are enforced by the state's planning authorities much more than guided by free market calculations. Moreover, the all-pervasive influence of the communist party in these countries shapes all decisions in a way, which, I hope, we shall never have to adopt in our countries.

In spite of all political differences between a communist one-party state and Western democracies, however, the Yugoslav economic system is a useful source of information on workers' interests and behaviour, because this system combines many elements of a market economy with a high degree of workers' self-management, although the workers are not owners of their firm's capital. Another useful source of experiences of workers' behaviour under conditions of parity co-determination is the West German coal and steel industry, in which workers' and shareholders' representatives have the same number of seats on the supervisory board of each company.

What can be learnt from the West German and the Yugoslav experiences? In West Germany a committee of experts (the 'Biedenkopf Committee') after extended hearings published a report on the working of parity participation in the coal and steel industries which essentially comes to similar conclusions as other investigations on this system of participation, namely, that it did not change entrepreneurial policy essentially (Deutscher Bundestag). According to this report employees' representatives on the board tended to identify their interests with those of the enterprise, and in many cases worker directors and shareholder directors finally voted for the same decisions. The considerabl improved information of trade unions on the financial situation of companies seems not to have led to increased wage demands. In some situations of financial crisis it seems even to have caused trade unions to make more moderate wage claims. From the behaviour and decisions of worker directors in these co-determined enterprises it must be concluded that they pursued a great number of aims, among them an improvement of work environment, of social institutions and of social security measures complementary to the state system of social insurance, reduction of working time, and alleviation of the financial and social hardships of employees losing employment in the firm. However, probably the most important objectives of their business policy were an increase in real wages and safety of jobs for the workers (Deutscher Bundestag, and Projektgruppe im WSI [1974]). These two objectives together imply that, far from a short-run maximisation of workers' income being the principal aim of German worker directors, it is the long-term maximisation of income in a viable and growing permanent enterprise.

In spite of the differences between German participation and Yugoslav self-management it is interesting to compare these conclusions with experiences recorded in Yugoslavia. Since Ward's famous essay (Ward [1958]), a number of models of the Yugoslav economy have been constructed which assume a very simple one-dimensional objective function, namely, maximisation of current income per worker, analogous to the conventional textbook hypothesis of profit maximisation for capitalist firms (Ward [1958], Dobias [1969] and Domar [1966]). In his painstaking efforts to find out what aims Yugoslav worker managers really have, Vanek [1970] rejects the Ward-Domar model of the Yugoslav self-management system. He says he never met 'anyone in Yugoslavia who could spell out in one word the object of his enterprise's pursuit, be it profit, steady income or volume of earnings. Consciously or not, everyone sees the enterprise as pursuing a large number of objectives of all kinds' (Vanek [1970] p. 171). He thinks that in view of this 'bewildering multiplicity' of objectives, the behaviour of self-managed firms cannot be explained by a simple, constant, one-dimensional objective function for all enterprises, but by different multidimensional and changing objective functions for different enterprises. Even Vanek, nevertheless, finds an increase of income and long-term existence of enterprises and their members among the most important objective variables of Yugoslav enterprises.

If that is true, Yugoslav as well as West German experience encourage me to assume the following for a preliminary and consciously simplifying theory of participation as the principal aims of co-determining workers and their representatives: long-run maximisation of income per worker, with safe jobs in a permanent enterprise. This implies that there is no justification for the widespread fear of opponents of self-management or participation that workers, in contrast to capitalists with their interest in the long-term growth of their capital, would rob their enterprises of all resources for investment in short-sighted greed for maximum immediate consumption.

But on the other hand there remains a wide area of conflicting interests between capitalists and workers. To find out the conflicts and harmonies of interests of both groups we should, I think, analyse in micro-economic decision models the kind of behaviour to be expected from the point of view of their group interests, then compare optimal solutions for both groups and finally try to draw conclusions on the kind of compromise decisions of the co-determined firm which seem most likely.

Conventional textbook micro-economics gives us solutions for the optimal behaviour of profit-maximising capitalists and of capitalists pursuing additional aims like growth, safety, power or independence. From their point of view this behaviour would remain optimal also under participation. In comparison with this 'capital-oriented' micro-economic theory, a 'labour-oriented' micro-economic theory explaining the decisions necessary for an optimal satisfaction of workers' aims is rather underdeveloped (Projektgruppe [1974] and WSI [1973]). Some progress towards such a theory has been made in connection with the analysis of the Yugoslav economic system and, to a lesser degree, in Germany for the analysis of co-determination. Decision models with different objective functions were constructed for the aims of maximisation of surplus value, of the absolute producers' income and of net income per worker (Dobias [1969], Domar [1966], Leipold [1974] and Ward [1958]). These models usually show considerable changes in optimal solutions for the instrument variables as a result of changes in objective functions. The most thoroughly analysed alternative to the conventional profit-maximising hypothesis is that of the Ward-Domar model: maximisation of net income per worker. Going from the world of profit-maximisation to Ward's Illyria one rather feels like Alice in Wonderland. In 'Illyria' reactions to changes in the prices of products and in factors of production, taxes and technology differ greatly from those in capitalist economies. It seems to depend very much on the type and the parameters of production functions whether syndicalist firms' supply functions of products and demand functions for factors of production are positively or negatively inclined. Abnormal, or inverse, destabilising reactions in the supply of products and the demand for factors of production to price changes become not only possible but likely. Monopolistic exploitation by increasing prices and reducing production would often be more profitable for self-managed workers than for profit-maximising Cournot-capitalists. Vanek says that, in the Ward model, 'the General-Director of a Post Office enterprise could satisfy the Maximisation rule by dismissing all the other employees and delivering one single letter at an infinite charge' (Vanek [1970] p. 141). An increase in fixed costs like, e.g., a lump sum tax would induce higher employment and production. Investments would generally be made in more capital-intensive processes than in capitalist enterprises.

My own experiments with models of this kind prove that behaviour in them is very sensitive to changes in production functions, cost functions and demand functions. It is not possible to say, generally, whether output of a single firm in Ward's 'Illyria' will *ceteris paribus* exceed that of a capitalist firm or be smaller. If, we may conclude, short-run maximisation of income per worker were the only objective of workers and short-run maximisation of capital profits that of capital-owners, the aims of these groups in co-determined firms would be strongly in conflict. Whether co-determined boards would be able to agree on a stable preference function which permitted an optimal or efficient solution, whether a mutual approximation to something like an Edgeworth contract curve (Stützel [1972]) could be expected, seems doubtful. If, however, both groups pursue long-term interests rather than short-term income maximisation aims, I would expect conflicts to be less radical.

German experiences with parity co-determination show that on the supervisory boards of German coal and steel companies worker directors and shareholder directors in many cases, although often only after long discussions, came to unanimous or almost unanimous decisions without having recourse to additional external pressures like strikes, and that in not a single important case was the vote of the 'neutral' director necessary in order to overcome a stalemate situation in a board's voting (Deutscher Bundestag). This does not, of course, prove an identity of interest. In spite of great differences between the interests of co-determining groups the probability of peaceful co-operation instead of open conflict here, as so often in economics, is increased by the fact that expected losses from conflicts with uncertain results are estimated to be higher than possible gains, and a negotiated trial-and-error approach to a stable solution which is sub-optimal for each group but Pareto-efficient becomes likely.

But even apart from these considerations there are strong indications that in Germany both co-determining groups did not find their interests completely irreconcilable. As soon as workers are concerned to secure employment and rising income in the long run in their present enterprises they, as much as capital-owners, want these enterprises to be permanent. Rather than slaughter the cow and eat it now they will prefer to feed and milk it. Moreover they quickly learn that in a competitive economy their enterprise, in order to survive in the market struggle, must grow by investing. And much as they may dislike the fact that, under continuing private ownership of capital, profits are accumulated by capitalists, they know that in this society profits are a necessary condition for investment. If they do not know it in the beginning they will quickly learn it the hard way by 'investment strikes' in recessions. Therefore, while opposed to profit maximisation, they will probably not attempt to reduce profits below the minimum level necessary for long-run growth of their enterprise. On the other hand capitalists will often prefer peaceful revenue-sharing the costs of strikes.

Maybe one of the main effects of participation in this respect will be the replacement of the old-fashioned labour-market struggle between management and trade unions by subtler, more rational forms of conflict-regulation behind the closed doors of supervisory boards. The Biedenkopf Report (Deutscher Bundestag) anyway, states explicitly that German worker-directors did not deny the necessity for their companies to make profits; and that improved information on the financial situation of their enterprises did not lead to an increase in wage demands, but that on the contrary, in some situations of financial crisis, it caused trade unions to make more moderate wage demands. In Yugoslavia, too little tendency towards the self-destruction of worker-managed enterprises through short-sighted group-egoism has been observed.

Even if the wish to uphold the level of employment of an enterprise were only a restriction to the objective of short-run maximisation of income of workers, it would prevent some of the most disturbing reactions of Ward's 'Illyria' model, namely the abnormal and destabilising decrease in employment and production as a reaction to price increases for products or price decreases for capital goods. Therefore, from this point of view the minimum employment restriction also reduces conflicts between workers' and capitalists' interests.

There remains, however, some divergence between capitalists' interest in the permanency of their enterprise, as long as it is more profitable than alternative capital investments, and the workers' interest in the permanent supply of employment and labour income by their enterprise; and the optimal amount of capital invested in the enterprise may be different from the point of view of the interests of the two groups.

In particular, we can assume that workers will always dislike a reduction in the employment of manpower due to insufficient demand or to labour-substituting technological changes, while for capitalists such a reduction is profitable. Increased resistance to downward adjustments of employment may increase dangers of 'overmanning', and resistance to upward adjustments of employment which would increase capital profits but not necessarily net revenue per worker may sometimes hamper the absorption of unemployed workers in periods of economic expansion. One should not, however, exaggerate these dangers, compared with those of the present system: trade unions, even without participation, nowadays successfully resist employment adjustments, and to German observers it seems that the degree of overmanning in British industries without participation is higher than in German industries with parity co-determination.

Moreover, the resistance of workers to dismissals is likely to be tempered by the partial conflict between their interests in long-run maximisation of income and in the maintenance of their jobs. If they see that inhibition of technical progress or inhibition of adjustments in employment to insufficient demand endangers the long-term viability of their enterprise they will presumably sacrifice the jobs of some of their colleagues now rather than lose all jobs in the future, although such a decision may only be possible after a long internal struggle between workers and their representatives on the board.

German experiences with parity co-determination, as observed by the Biedenkopf Committee and others, confirm this expectation: so far no systematic attempt to prevent technical progress in the interest of employment or to bias it in some labour-using direction has been reported. In recessions resistance to mass releases of workers has usually led only to postponements of employment reductions. The employees' representatives concentrated their efforts rather on 'social plans' intended to regulate dismissals and grant financial compensation to released employees.

It seems likely, however, that the mild forms of resistance to employment reduction in the German coal and steel industries were to some degree a consequence of very favourable circumstances in the past. During the long periods of full employment and over-full employment in the fifties and sixties in Germany, workers who became redundant in one industry had no difficulty in finding a new and often better job elsewhere. Moreover, in coalmines the proportion of miners who wanted to give up their dangerous and hard work was always very high. Recently, with high rates of increasingly lasting unemployment, workers fight much harder against reductions in employment. There is the example of the Volkswagenwerk, where workers' representatives together with shareholders' representatives (who depend politically on the trade unions) have gained some kind of majority influence on the board.

They have used this influence to postpone investment decisions and unavoidable employment reductions far too long, and have thereby aggravated the Volkswagenwerk's dangerous crisis. This behaviour may well set a more realistic pattern for future decisions than the relatively harmonious climate in employment crises of co-determined firms in the past. It seems that in Yugoslavia, as in Germany, downward adjustments of employment are achieved only with great difficulty.

One aspect of an enterprise's investment policy which is likely to become more controversial, in my opinion, is investment abroad. Capitalists who expect higher profit rates from investments in foreign countries and who would prefer to invest there are likely to meet increased resistance from co-determining workers who, in the interests of their jobs, will try to direct investment to home factories. Again, the recent resistance of Volkswagenwerk workers' representatives to move production of their cars for the American market to the USA may serve as an example of such a tendency, which has become stronger in Germany since a series of revaluations of the DM has made low-wage countries more attractive for German investors.

Even movements of capital between different regions of one country will, as experience in Yugoslavia in particular shows, meet opposition from workers who fear for their jobs or are not inclined to migrate interregionally. The international and interregional mobility and efficiency of capital could thus be reduced.

Complete or almost complete identity of interests between co-determining workers and capitalists will, I fear, strengthen the market power of their enterprises by monopolistic exploitation. Their ideas on the exact volume of optimal output or on optimal prices may differ, but both will profit from limitation of competition. The workers' delegates on the boards of the German coal and steel industries have certainly never shown any enthusiasm for the neo-liberals' ideals of perfect competition. On the contrary, they have faithfully supported the capital-owners in their fight for a re-concentration of their industries and for administrative discrimination against foreign competition. Generally, if participation permits workers to take a considerable share of profits from monopoly, their interest as producers in small outputs and high prices for their firms will always be stronger than their interest as consumers in large outputs and low prices. I fear very much that the introduction of a general system of parity co-determination could further weaken the already half-hearted struggle against monopolies. In any case the danger of the exploitation of consumers by producers in a syndicalist system – foreseen already by Austro-Marxists like e.g., Bauer [1921] and Korsch [1969] – is no less relevant for participatory systems.

Another danger I foresee is that the pressure for government subsidies, import controls and import duties on competing foreign products which is in the interests of both workers and capitalists will be strengthened under participation. For Germany this danger is well documented by the formidable united pressure groups of workers and capitalists in the coal and steel industries in the past.

There is a good deal of speculation that participating or self-managing workers would prefer investments with smaller risks and uncertainties and thereby hamper fundamental innovations, but in my opinion neither German nor Yugoslav experience can corroborate this theory conclusively.

I feel that all these approaches to some problems of a micro-economic analysis of co-determined firms are still preliminary, unsatisfactory and vague and can do no more than suggest the direction in which all these problems should be further investigated in order to develop a micro-economic theory of participation.

TOTAL MICRO-ECONOMIC ANALYSIS OF PARTICIPATION

Only on the basis of a sufficiently reliable theory of the behaviour of co-determined firms can we see how participation will affect the overall performance of a market economy. Since I am so uncertain as to how co-determined firms will behave I cannot propose a satisfactory total micro-economic, or even just a macro-economic, theory of the overall effects of participation.

We certainly can say that in those simple models of self-managed economies which assume maximisation of income per worker as the only objective of enterprises a rather terrifying picture of the interdependent market processes is implied. Even under conditions of perfect competition in markets for products and non-labour factors of production nothing like general static Pareto-efficiency will be achieved. Because, in such a system, labour input and income is not a cost factor to be minimised in any efficient combination of factors of production but (as labour income per worker) an objective variable to be maximised, the firm's definition and calculation of costs excludes elements of costs which should be included in any calculation of social costs. The monetary values of the marginal products of labour will be different for different firms in equilibrium. The ratio of physical marginal products of different factors of production will not be the same for all firms, and there is no tendency towards an equalisation of labour income per worker throughout the economy. Firms that have realised the level of employment which guarantees maximum income per capita have no incentive to employ currently unemployed workers or those who work in enterprises which pay much lower wages. Therefore no automatic price-regulated tendencies towards full employment can be expected, and functional as well as personal distribution of income could have an unpleasant degree of inequality. Internationally, movements towards an equalisation of factor prices are improbable. To these impediments to a static efficient allocation of society's productive means must be added the dynamic dangers of 'abnormal' reactions of supply and demand that can destabilise markets.

If we replace the only aim of income maximisation per worker by the multi-dimensional long-run objective function which I believe parity co-determined firms will have, I would not expect participation to result in such a scene of totally uneconomical and wildly fluctuating markets. Even the Yugoslav self-management system is far from being disastrous, although — with some unemployment, large differences in income between enterprises, industries and regions, and unsatisfactory elasticities of adjustment to changes – it shows some of the unattractive features of this model.

efficiency

Moreover, one might object, even without participation present market economies are so far away from the utopia of general Pareto-efficiency that it does not really matter whether participation is added to monopolistic market elements, differences between private and social marginal costs or state interventions and other factors disturbing the conditions for efficiency. In order to condemn participation from the point of view of economic efficiency it is also not sufficient to prove that equilibrium under participation is not Pareto-efficient: it would be necessary to show that in comparison with the present system it increases inefficiencies. One could also reject conclusions from static models of participatory economies by pointing out that dynamic functions of workable competition are more important than the static functions of realising short-run efficiency.

social conflict

I cannot supply such a complete general dynamic and micro-economic theory of participation, and am therefore in rather a weak position to answer these objections. If my presumptions on behaviour patterns under participation are correct I must say that I see one likely improvement in the working of our market system: a smoother regulation of social conflicts. I am not sure whether to this advantage that of a stronger motivation of workers to work more productively can be added. (Voigt [1962] Weddigen [1962]). I see, on the other hand, dangers of a nationally and internationally less efficient combination of factors of production, and the adverse effects of higher degrees of monopoly, of overmanning and of less elastic adjustments to changes in market conditions. I do not take these dangers lightly: I would not exclude the possibility that for our economic system already strained by inconsistent and stupid interferences of government, trade unions and 'pluralistic' associations of all kinds in the market process, parity co-determination will prove to be just that burden under which the market system collapses or deteriorates so much that we would do better to replace it by some completely different non-market system which – I am afraid – might at the same time be one without effective workers' participation and economic 'democracy'.

ECONOMIC POLICY IN CO-DETERMINED MARKET ECONOMIES

Because I do not know a satisfactory economic theory of a participatory economy I do not yet know how economic policy for given economic aims should be changed. Only of one thing can we be sure: the more extremely the behaviour of co-determined enterprises changes and the more differently they react to prices, taxes, interest rates, state expenditure, etc., the more will radical changes in the political instruments for the traditional objectives of economic policy become necessary.

In Ward's self-management model, for example, enterprises react to increases in interest rates with an expansion of production, not with a reduction as we would expect in capitalist enterprises; and a decrease in a lump sum tax would induce enterprises to reduce production instead of having a neutral effect as in short-run micro-economic models of capitalist firms.

Traditional macro-economic decision models would, because of changing responses of objective variables to instrument variables, be useless. The unsatisfactory experiments with macro-economic state policy in Yugoslavia demonstrate that, the more behaviour under participation deviates from capitalist patterns, the more probable it is that both the whole 'distribution of labour' between market powers, on which we rely for the regulating of micro-structures, and state intervention for regulating the macro-aggregates in the circular flow of income will have to be reconsidered. I do not have the impression that advocates of parity co-determination are aware of this problem.

Parity co-determination, I conclude, is a social experiment with uncertain economic results. Apart from its political advantages we can economically risk this experiment, but only if we are flexible enough and politically strong and courageous enough to adjust our economic policies to its yet uncertain necessities, or, if necessary, stop the experiment in time. If an economic system of parity co-determination is introduced, great, and hitherto unsolved, tasks of explaining it theoretically and of designing strategies for its regulation are waiting for economists.

REFERENCES

Bauer, O. [1921], *Der Weg zum Sozialismus* (Wien).
Biedenkopf, K. [1972], *Mitbestimmung* (Köln).
Deutscher Bundestag, Sachverständigenkommission (Biedenkopf-Kommission), *Mitbestimmung in Unternehmen, Bericht der Sachverständigen-kommission zur Auswertung der bisherigen Erfahrung bei der Mitbestimmung*, Deutscher Bundestag – 6 Wahlperiode, Drucksache VI, 334.
Dobias, Peter [1969], *Das jugoslawische Wirtschaftssystem, Entwicklung und Wirkungsweise* (Tübingen).
Domar, E. L. [1966], 'The Soviet Collective Farm as a Producer Cooperative', *American Economic Review*, 56, S.736–57.

Gutmann, G. [1968], 'Bruttoeinkommensprinzip und öffentliches Eigentum. Ein ordnungstheoretisches Problem der Marktanpassung', *Ordo*, 19 Band. S.257 ff.

Korsch, K. [1969], *Schriften zur Sozialisierung* (Frankfurt am Main).

Koubek, N. Müller, H. D., Schiebe-Lange, I. (eds), [1974], *Betriebswirtschaftliche Probleme der Mitbestimmung* (Frankfurt am Main).

Leipold, H. [1974], *Betriebsdemokratie–ökonomische Systemrationalität* (Stuttgart).

Projektgruppe im WSI [1974], *Grundelemente einer Arbeitsorientierten Einzelwirtschaftslehre* (Köln) WSI–Studien No. 33.

Seidel, Heinz [1973], 'Die Notwendigkeit ausserbetrieblicher Arbeitnehmervertreter im mitbestimmten Aufsichtsrat', *Gewerkschaftliche Monatshefte*, 10, 73 (Köln), S.176 ff.

Stützel, W. [1972], *Wert, Preis und Macht* (Aalen).

Vanek, J. [1971], *The Participatory Economy: an Evolutionary Hypothesis and a Strategy for Development* (Ithaca).

Vanek, J. [1970], *The General Theory of Labor Managed Market Economies* (Ithaca).

Voigt, F. [1962], 'Die Mitbestimmung der Arbeitnehmer in den Unternehmungen', in *Zur Theorie und Praxis der Mitbestimmung* (Berlin).

Wagner, M. [1972], 'Funktionen von "Einkommen" und "Gewinn" im Wirtschaftssystem Jugoslawiens', in K. P. Hensel, K. Wesseley and K. Wagner, *Das Profitprinzip – seine ordnungspolitischen Alternativen in sozialistischen Wirtschaftssystemen* (Stuttgart) S.134 ff.

Ward, Benjamin [1958], 'The Firm in Illyria: Market Syndicalism', *American Economic Review*, 48 (chapter 1 of this volume).

Weddigen, O. [1962], *Begriff und Produktivität der betrieblichen Mitbestimmung* (Berlin).

Wirtschafts-und Sozialwissenschaftliches Institut, WSI (ed.) [1973], *Arbeitsorientierte Einzelwirtschaftslehre contra Kapitalorientierte Betriebswirtschaftslehre* (Köln) WSI–Studien No. 24.

5 Workers' Councils in the Prague Spring of 1968

Jiří Kosta

A shortened version of a study prepared for the Bundesinstitut für ostwissenschaftliche und internationale Studien, Cologne, in August 1975

1 ECONOMIC REFORM AND THE PROCESS OF DEMOCRATISATION (1965–8)[1]

The Czechoslovak economic reform began about three years before the Prague Spring of 1968. The initial steps were in their impact on the decision-making institutions guided by technocratic considerations. In 1966 and 1967 a large proportion of the centrally fixed planning targets (production targets, manpower, investments) were suspended and greater powers of decision were granted to individual enterprises; the orders of the planning bureaucracy were replaced by economic policy instruments and indicative targets emanating from the centre; there was a change of direction from the fetishism of quantity to efficiency criteria; but in spite of all these improvements, the majority of workers were still excluded from the economic decision-making process.

It was only from the beginning of 1968, when the general process of democratisation made possible by a change of political leadership began to affect Czechoslovak society as a whole, that the technocratic type of economic reform was transformed within a few months to a reform concept based on democratic participation.

Decentralisation as practised during the interim period (1965-early 1968) was at the time and in the circumstances the only available option. The established political leadership around Novotný was still able to maintain its control even if by somewhat different methods than previously, and this in spite of the growing economic crisis of the early 1960s, for which the public held them responsible. They disguised their vested interest in the continuance of their rule with slogans such as 'the leading role of the party in the economy' and, in order to prevent workers' control in the plants, the 'incompatibility of group property with socialism'. The transitional period was also required so that the anti-bureaucratic opposition's intellectuals and workers could undergo a learning process to enable them to overcome the dogmas of Stalinism.

Finally, doubts among the public about the practical feasibility of workers' participation were predominant in the beginning of the reform period.

The demand for participatory workers' councils in plants and enterprises (this institution will be studied in the ensuing pages) came from two directions in the early months of 1968. First from groups of experts, and after a time lag, but eventually with much greater force, from blue and white-collar workers in the industry. Initially certain scholars, especially economists, sociologists and political scientists, stressed that the reforms, as hitherto undertaken, to decentralise the economic system had amounted on the one hand to a loosening of the monopoly of bureaucratic control; but that on the other hand there had been a change in the form rather than the substance of power, the complete abolition of which was a necessary goal for a free socialist society.

It is true that in the early months of 1968 the protagonists of participation were guided by differing conceptions, ranging from a model based primarily on technocratic elements through compromises between technocratic and democratic principles of management to a fully-fledged workers' control concept in line with the leftist traditions of the workers' movement (Pravda [1975] pp. 1–5). Among the majority the view finally prevailed that the hierarchy of economic decision-makers, a chain of command stretching from Ministers through managing directors and executives down to rank-and-file workers, would have to be smashed, and that the 'workers' collective should exert influence upon the management of the enterprise' (Právo [1968]). This concept won the approval of the new party leadership under Dubček. The action programme of the Czechoslovakian Communist Party of April 1968, in which the results of these discussions are laid down, speaks of 'democratic organs within enterprises' to which 'the directors and leading executives of the undertaking are responsible for the total results of their work' (Právo [1968]). The programme also affirms the principle of election to these bodies from the rank-and-file members of the plant as well as from representatives of outside interests.

Within weeks there were moves towards the formation of workers' councils in some plants. They originated from various groups and institutions, in some cases from trade union branches, in others from the plant organisations of the Communist Party and in some instances from spontaneously-formed action groups. Simultaneously the party leadership under Dubček and the central council of the trade unions were engaged in evolving a concept of participation which would not confine spontaneous action within too narrow limits while also meeting problems arising in the enterprises according to reasonable forms of workers' control. Public discussion in the press, on radio and television – here journalists played a crucial role – and debate inside the party and trade union movement, in which account was taken of the experience of Czechoslovak post-war works councils and of information about the Yugoslav system of industrial self-management, produced the Government decree of 6 June 1968, in which 'provisional guidelines for the constitution and control of collective bodies of democratic administration and decision-making organs in enterprises' were laid down. This edict became an integral part of a comprehensive declaration of the central council of trade unions of July 1968 on the whole subject of industrial self-management. [2] These decisions also paved the way for the formation of workers' councils on a broad front.

In the first phase of the debate on self-government (February-May 1968) workers in the plants had maintained a waiting attitude, but after June 1968 the situation changed rapidly. Especially after the July declaration of the trade unions it became obvious that workers and employees were giving their active support and displaying growing initiative. The attitude of directors and managing executives was more ambiguous. Those especially whose promotion had been due to their willingness to obey rather than to their ability opposed the workers' council movement; some of them had to face the fact that after the establishment of councils they were not confirmed in their managing positions. Yet others amongst the more highly qualified managers were sympathetic to the workers' participation, for they expected to get more support and less petty interference from them than had been the case under conditions of bureaucratically centralised planning. A third group of leading executives, the ever-adaptable ones, remained cautious and waiting. The reluctant attitude on the part of some of the Ministerial bureaucracy and the partly negative disposition of many directors and managers only served to reinforce the wave of sympathy for the idea of industrial self-government among workers and employees in factories and plants.

The most enthusiastic advocates of the concept of workers' councils were to be found above all among the more highly qualified strata of blue and white-collar workers, among a number of active trade unionists and among many ordinary members of the basic organisations of the Communist Party.

The Invasion of Czechoslovakia by Warsaw Pact troops on 21 August 1968 took place during this remarkable upsurge of the workers' council movement in the factories. The factories became the points of strongest resistance against the intervention, and it was just this new situation which, after the first shock was absorbed, caused an acceleration in the development of workers' councils in industry. On the surface this appeared to be a paradox of this period, in fact it was a logical consequence of events: at the very moment when the Soviet leadership (only a few days after the invasion) demanded amongst its earliest political requirements a suspension of the workers' councils there arose in the factories an even stronger spontaneous drive in favour of the councils.

At the beginning of the year 1969 there were in the country about a hundred and twenty workers' councils which had been set up mainly in industrial enterprises, especially in engineering works.[3] These councils represented about a fifth of the workers in the secondary sector of the economy. Even after the change of leadership in the party in April 1969, the replacement of Dubček by Husák, the workers' councils spread like wildfire in spite of all initially cautious attempts to put the brake on. The movement reached its climax in July 1969 when, according to Czechoslovak estimates, about 300 workers' councils and 300 preparatory committees for the establishment of councils had been constituted in Czechoslavak enterprises (Pravda [1975] p. 9).

The increasing identification of the population with the concept of self-government is borne out by a poll conducted in the summer of 1968 and repeated in the spring of 1969 by the Institute for Opinion Research.[4] The replies of more than 1600 representative citizens to the question 'In your opinion, was the establishment of workers' councils in all big enterprises useful or not?' gave the following results.

	July 1968	March 1969
Yes	53.3%	59.1%
No	9.9%	3.0%

The remainder of those questioned were somewhat more qualified or uncertain in their answers. In any case the proportion of those who were clearly opposed to the councils was reduced from 10 per cent in the summer of 1968 to 3 per cent in the spring of 1969.

Those members of the technocracy and bureaucracy who had treated the concept of workers' councils from the beginning with scepticism were as early as the autumn of 1968 attempting to 'cleanse' the idea of participation of its elements of self-government in order to 'save it'. In line with this development there had crept into the attitude of the Czech and Slovak governments to the as yet incomplete legislative proposals a 'technocratic' variant of the workers' council constitution. Instead of permitting workers to form a majority of the councils, these official proposals reduced rank-and-file personnel to a minority, by including directors, representatives of the State administration and other public institutions. The surviving clique of functionaries of the Novotný era refused to accept any form of councils, either those started in 1968 as workers' councils or those which were at the beginning of 1969 more cautiously designated enterprise councils. The demands of the Soviet leadership, which were supported by this numerically weak group of ultras, had finally to be accepted by the new party leadership in the summer of 1969. The legislative proposals were withdrawn and the existing councils in the factories liquidated. This 'normalisation process' was accomplished as part of 'self-criticism' and 'self-liquidation', but this did not change the fact that it was prepared, initiated and its completion ensured from above. In the repressive atmosphere of the purges which were now beginning, there was no possibility of resisting the dissolution of the councils which had been laid down from on high. The fate of the workers' council movement was sealed through the self-liquidation of the biggest and most important council in the country, the workers' council of the Škoda works in Plzeň on 12 November 1969.

2 DECISION-MAKING INSTITUTIONS IN THE PARTICIPATION MODEL OF 1968

2.1 Institutional regulations[5]

We now turn to the institutional regulations for workers' councils laid down by the decision of the Czechoslovak trade unions of July 1968 mentioned earlier, especially their composition and powers, and also the newly-defined functions of the other more important decision-makers within enterprises, the management, the trade union and party organisations. It has to be remembered that the document of the trade unions deals with the organisational structure only by way of recommendation and does not lay down obligatory guidelines, and that specific institutions are only very vaguely defined. The reason for not making the framework obligatory was that it was initially a question of proceeding by trial and error, so that on the basis of this experience, definitive institutional regulations could be laid down in the legislative proposals which were in course of preparation. The relevant law on the constitution of enterprises was due to be passed early in 1969.

One recommendation was to elect the majority of council members in direct and secret elections from among all (blue and white-collar) workers of the enterprise. Representatives of outside interest groups and institutions should join the council according to the circumstances of the enterprise. Such outside representatives might be independent experts, representatives of supplier or customer enterprises, general consumers, state or regional organs, banks granting credit, etc. It was to be remembered that, under the existing structure of property rights, there was no question of including private persons or institutions. The total membership should be between 10 and 30 persons according to the size of the enterprise. It was recommended that membership should be for a relatively long period of about four to six years with a half or a third of the members retiring after two years.

As against the Yugoslav system of self-government under which the director is a mere executant of the decisions of the workers' councils, the Czechoslovak concept set out in the government and trade union documents provides for a division of functions between the two institutions, council and management. The function of controlling the management, however, remains with the council. The directors are appointed, as in Yugoslavia, by the workers' council. The workers' council, however, has full powers of decision in only three important matters: first, as already mentioned, the appointment and dismissal of the director, and on his nomination, the deputy directors; secondly, the salaries and bonuses of the directors; thirdly, the question of the continuation, merging or division of the enterprise.

It is recommended that the council should have wide consultative powers ('the workers' council makes a judgement') in the following matters: (a) the development of the enterprise and related planning of investment; (b) the principles according to which the income of the enterprise (profit) is to be distributed, such principles to be embodied in collective contracts between the trade union organisation and the management; (c) questions of organisation and articles of incorporation of the enterprise; and lastly, (d) in matters on the final balance sheet of the enterprise. In all these questions, however, the final powers of decision are apparently to be reserved to the managing director. In other respects, too, a relatively large area of discretion is left to the management within the framework of its task of directing. The director is responsible for the development and sales policy of the undertaking, he organises the preparation and execution of the process of production and he makes decisions on all current technical, commercial, financial and personnel questions.

In opting for this division of functions between council and management the argument prevailed that there were various reasons for not allowing a too wide and detailed power of decision to the workers' councils in the running of an enterprise. It was the opinion of a number of reputable economists that successful economic performance required immediate and specialist decision-making in all current problems. This could be more appropriately performed by the management apparatus, if always under the control of the collective organs of the enterprise, rather than by the organs of self-government.

The government and trade union document mentions two possible alternatives: 1. membership of managers in the workers' council; 2. the incompatibility of management functions with membership. In this, as in other not clearly worked out regulations, the view prevailed that in cases of disagreement it could only be practical experience which would show up the most favourable solution. The position was similar in the case of the somewhat ambiguous regulation of the right of the councils to be consulted on the various questions mentioned earlier (only in case of conflict over investment decisions were more detailed procedures laid down – 'a right of veto after repeated debate where it was a matter of excessively risky projects which could endanger the appropriate salary and wage development').

Finally, precise conditions were established for the dismissal of a director as well as for a period of office for directors of at least six years. This was done in the interests of the permanent stability of the enterprise and as a protection against unjustified dismissals of managers, perhaps because of necessary but unpopular measures. The appointment of the director should be on the basis of public advertisement taking into consideration professional, political and human qualifications.

The role of the trade unions was redefined, for up to now they had been more or less an appendage of the party and had the task within the enterprise of working with the management and the party organisation towards the fulfilment of the plan. The primary task of the trade union organisation was now to be the regulation of wage and salary conditions of employees. Although the document envisaged close co-operation of the trade unions with the workers' councils, there was also a clear division of functions. The main task of the council was to collaborate with the management which it had appointed and which it controlled, in other words with the long-term concept of the enterprise. Against this, the main task of the trade unions was the care of the social situation of the workers in the enterprise. This task of the trade union organisation was to find its concrete expression in the collective contracts between the management and the trade unions.

There is no mention in these documents of the relationship of the workers' council to the basic organisations of the Communist Party within the enterprise. During the Prague Spring, new principles were formulated according to which the party was to be in future no longer a substitute for other organisations in society and no longer the universal administrator of society (Právo [1968] p. 297f.). Under these principles the workers' councils together with the management would become sovereign decision-makers independent of the party on the level of the enterprise except with respect to the government's planning and economic organs. The organs of the party were to be regarded as educational institutions whose task was to win for their members and for the public in general the long-term aims of a democratic socialism.

2.2 Problems and trends in the Czechoslovak workers' councils

In spite of their short existence the councils of the years 1968 and 1969 gave rise to some problems and showed some trends which are worthy of note:

(a)   Over-representation of highly skilled professional groups
In free elections which had not been manipulated by any power groups
or lobbies, more than 70 per cent of those elected were technicians,
about 25 per cent workers; the remainder were other professional
groups, in the main ordinary administrative employees. Even amongst
the small number of workers' representatives, the proportion of highly
skilled specialist workers predominated so that the large category of less
skilled workers and ancillary workers was hardly represented at all
(Kosta [1973] p. 21f.).

This composition of the council deserves consideration. The pre-
dominance of white collar personnel had specific causes. The workers
regarded the party and the economic bureaucracy of the 1950s as a
group of loud-mouths and incompetents. It was an open secret that in
the Novotný era within the hierarchical planning mechanism there
prevailed an inverse proportion between qualification and position. The
more important the function, the lower was the qualification. Amongst
the widest section of the population there was a real desire to entrust the
direction of the productive process once more to real specialists. Thus in
free elections a relatively large number of technicians, of whom some
were originally skilled workers, were elected to the councils. It is obvious
that this composition of the participatory bodies carried with it certain
dangers for the future, especially in view of the long period of office of
council members of about four years; there was likely to be a tendency
for the new technocrats to become independent of the enterprise
collective, so that the original intentions of participation would be
nullified.

(b)   Disproportion between the number of employees and the number of
      council members (Pravda [1975] pp. 12–13)
Enterprises employing several thousand workers were not uncommon,
since a high degree of concentration in Czechoslovak industry was
artificially fostered by administrative monopoly. Therefore it was by no
means rare for one member of the workers' council to represent several
hundred members of the enterprise. It is hardly open to dispute that in
this way alienation could arise between even the most trustworthy
functionaries and the collective body of employees. It must be admitted,
however, that this initial disproportion between the small number on the
workers' council and the large number of employees could have led to
the establishment of more councils in separate enterprises and plants in
large-scale industry, if the experiment had lasted longer. From the
Yugoslav experience it could be foreseen that new problems of co-
ordination would arise between the overall council at the enterprise level
and the subordinate council in separate plants.

(c)   *Under-representation of external interest groups* (Pravda [1975] p. 16)

In opposition to the guidelines laid down by the government and the trade unions, it became noticeable that when workers' councils were being established, there was a reluctance to include representatives of groups external to the enterprise. The idea of representing outside institutions was not in principle discarded but in practice the attempt was made to keep the number of members from outside the enterprise as low as possible. In so far as it was a question of including highly qualified experts, the functionaries of the councils as well as other influential groups in the enterprise attempted to induce the management to conclude consultative contracts with such experts rather than to include them as full members in the council.

(d)   *Activities of the workers' council* (Fišera [1970])

Only in some traditional enterprises did the opinion prevail amongst workers that it was the main task of the council to deal with the question of wages. Increasingly, the opinion gained ground amongst the public that it was the job of the council to take account, not merely of the short-term, but at least in equal measure of the long-term interests of the collective group of employees. An opinion poll of March 1969 showed that of the questions to be dealt with, the wider public gave slightly greater importance to problems of management and production, ahead of social and wage questions, while the workers were for a certain balance between these two issues.

A survey conducted in January 1969 among members of 103 councils is even more revealing about the relative importance of proposals which were actually discussed within their councils. The following problems took up the first five positions out of thirty-eight:

(i) Long-term production plan and annual plans of the enterprise — 3058 proposals;
(ii) Long-term economic plan of the enterprise and plants — 3000 proposals;
(iii) Investment policy of the enterprise — 2981 proposals;
(iv) Annual accounting of the production plan of the enterprise — 2874 proposals;
(v) Concept and accounting of the financial policy of the enterprise — 2854 proposals.

In comparing the two surveys, the conclusion seems justified that the elected representatives were more conscious of their long-term tasks as entrepreneurs than were the workers who had elected them.

(e)   *Distribution of power between workers' councils and management* (Pravda [1975] pp. 13–15)

Even in the previous section (*d*) a divergence from the officially approved model of participation was apparent in the distribution of power between workers' councils and management. Instead of the envisaged compromise between self-governing and management principles, questions of policy affecting the enterprise in fact bulked large in the activity of the councils. The problem arises whether the councils confined themselves to maintaining the right of consultation and of judgement allocated to them or whether they did not themselves take certain decisions or preliminary decisions. As the period of experimentation was so short and evidence is insufficient, no definite conclusion is possible. There is much to be said for the view that, as Pravda declared (Pravda [1975] p. 14), many of the workers' councils followed the trend-setting workers' council of the greatest steel and engineering works in Czechoslovakia, the Škoda works in Plzeň. The council acted on the guideline that the workers' councils were competent to make decisions on all basic questions of policy affecting the enterprise and that the management were regarded as mere executants of this policy. This should not mean, it was stressed, that the council ought to occupy itself with day-to-day problems of production technique or with economic details. These would be matters for the management and their expert staffs.

Although a tendency may have asserted itself in the short period of experiment, it remains one of the most difficult problems of any sort of workers' council to establish a sensible relationship between the decisions of the management necessary for reasons of time and expertise and a desire to ensure workers' participation in decision-making, the legitimacy of which will be investigated in the next section.

(*f*) *Workers' councils and trade union and party organisations* (Pravda [1975] pp. 17–21)

A definitive judgement is again not possible about the relationship between the newly-constituted workers' councils with the trade union and party organisations, owing to the brief existence of the system of participation. There are a few indications that the workers' councils managed on the whole to collaborate well with the trade unions, even if it was not always possible to limit the trade union organisations (according to the guidelines) only to social questions affecting the employees.

No clear trend emerges from the information about the relationship of the councils to the party units. This may be connected with the fact that the situation varied from enterprise to enterprise. Nevertheless more than 52 per cent of the elected representatives on the workers' councils or on the preparatory committees for the establishment of councils were members of the Communist Part. This high proportion of party members in the councils does not alter the fact that in a number of plants party functionaries were denied membership in the workers' council or were debarred from their meetings. This apparent contradiction is probably to be explained by the fact that in the first case it was a question of ordinary members of the party whereas in the latter case of exclusion functionaries of the old type were concerned. It is difficult to estimate how the relationship between party organisations and workers' councils would have developed in the longer term.

3 PARTICIPATION AND PLANNING

The first two sections were concerned with the empirical development of workers' councils in the Prague Spring and only touched on some general problems. In this section, it is the intention to raise some more general problems arising from the discussions and experiences of the Czechoslovak experiment. The crucial point of concern is the problem of the divergence of interests in a socialist society and the relationship of participation to planning. The more general problems of workers' participation outside industry is largely ignored here because it goes beyond the theme of this paper. Before we turn to these questions, let us give a brief reflection on participation as a means and as an end.

3.1 Participation as means and objective

Participation can be taken either as a means towards the fulfilment of other aims or as an objective in itself; in fact, these two dimensions are not always clearly separate.

Participation in decision-making is seen by many supporters of a 'democratisation of the economy' as a means to an end, principally that of economic efficiency. Arguments of this kind played a part in the Czechoslovak reform discussions of the years 1967 and 1968, coming especially from academic economists. A number of economists who had advocated in the years 1964 to 1967 a more coherent decentralisation of the system of planning and control gradually moved from a technocratic variant of reform towards the participatory concept. Their arguments were as follows: an identification of the employees with their enterprise brought about by participation would favour a short-term and long-term motivation of every worker towards a more efficient development of the enterprise. It was frequently stressed that participation in decision-making would need to be coupled to a certain extent with a participation of profits.

Besides, participation was often regarded as an overriding aim especially by Marxist philosophers and other social scientists. In contrast to the power of capital in the West and bureaucratisation of the socialist states in the East, the self-determination of producers will, it was argued, open the way to a classless, domination-free society. This line of reasoning, advanced by a number of Czechoslovak philosophers, political scientists and sociologists under the influence of the Yugoslav group 'Praxis', increasingly gained ground in the factories. This probably helped the transformation, mentioned earlier, of moves towards participation into concepts of self-government.

Both the instrumental and the normative argument for participation furnished proof of the legitimacy of this aspiration.

3.2   Conflicts of interest and participation[6]

We are advancing the thesis that workers' participation offers a means of solving clashes of interests. This is true both of the instrumental and the normative argument about participation, as will be shown below.

The Czechoslovak Spring of 1968 saw a reform movement in which the overwhelming majority of the population opposed the bureaucratic monopoly of power by a minority in all areas of society. The omnipotence of the central organs had already been loosened through the previous decentralisation of planning. But the conflict between the decision-making élites, the composition of which had changed and the number of which had increased, on the one side, and the working people excluded from decision-making, on the other side, had not, as already pointed out, been solved by economic reform. The establishment of workers' councils within enterprises undoubtedly constituted a decisive step towards the elimination of this conflict of interests within society.

The fundamental conflict of interests between the decision-makers and those excluded from decision-making is a consequence of the 'Soviet-type' political system and is not conditioned by any objective external pressures. The history of this system of domination is rooted in the circumstances of the Russian revolution of 1917 and of the years immediately following and is conditioned by a series of specific influences of that period, through backwardness and shortages, through the decimation of the working class in the civil war, through the necessity for rapid capital accumulation in the Soviet economy and so on.[7] But we must agree with Deutscher and Šik when they criticise the absence of a process of democratisation in the Soviet Union after the difficulties of the first post-revolution years had been overcome (Deutscher [1967] pp. 40–9). One cannot justify the transfer of the Soviet-type decision-making to Czechoslovakia, a country with a numerically strong, politically conscious working class, a well-qualified and progressive technical and economic intelligentsia, with a mature industrial base and sufficient democratic traditions.

The conflict within a political system between a minority of decision-makers and a majority excluded from decision-making can only be removed through a comprehensive process of democratisation in society, however difficult to achieve this may be. The basis of democratisation in the economy is the participation in decisions in the workplace and in the enterprise. This required process of democratisation, of which the most important component was the establishment of workers' councils, is a way of overcoming the fundamental contradiction between an élitist minority and the overwhelming majority of the population. Workers' participation in this context is to be regarded as an objective which should bring about the removal of existing structures of domination.

In a socialist society there exists, however, apart from this fundamental contradiction of a system of bureaucratic state socialism, objectively conditioned specific-interest conflicts which cannot be removed through a change in the political system. These objective conflicts are, however, not to be taken as absolute facts for all time, nor is it necessary to accept their intensity. It is a matter of alleviating them as far as possible. At issue are three types of interest divergences:

1. conflicts within the enterprise;
2. conflicts between separate enterprises;
3. conflicts between enterprise and society.

Within an enterprise, there is a divergence of interest between the individual and the enterprise as a whole. To put it concretely, it is a conflict between the short-term wage interests and the long-term investment interests of the members of the enterprise (Sik [1968]). It is often argued that members of an enterprise collective are more concerned to maximise their wages than to take care of investment, since they are not necessarily in a position to enjoy the future fruits of investment activities, partly for reasons of age and partly because they will change their place of work.

And yet, workers' participation would seem to offer the best chance, in spite of this undoubted clash of interests, that the members of an enterprise, presumably in the course of a gradual learning process, will identify with their enterprise and will, therefore, develop such a long-term view of their interest. Initially, it is possible for the management, as well as for the external representatives on a workers' council, as was foreseen in the guidelines, to form a certain counterweight against decisions based on short-term considerations. Moreover, the early experience in Czechoslovakia has shown that the representatives of the workers in the councils were by no means solely concerned for a higher distribution of wages. They have shown an understanding for the need of investment in an enterprise. In our opinion, one should not underestimate the possibility of developing a solidarity of consciousness amongst workers and employees which is trained through long-term common tasks.

Conflicts of interest between enterprises on the one hand and society on the other are more fully discussed in the following section. Here we have to point out once more that in the Czechoslovak participation model, the reduction of conflicts was to have been facilitated by the representation on the workers' councils of groups from outside and 'above' the actual plants. Representatives from outside the enterprises consisted of partners with opposing interests such as suppliers, customers and those participating in investment. Representatives from above the enterprise consisted of consumers, regional, environmental and other social interests. If in practice it was the case that there was a reluctance by those within the enterprise to admit representatives of outside interests, this proves clearly the existence of conflicts of interest for the reduction of which appropriate means have to be developed.

3.3   Conflicts of interest and economic reform

Divergences of interest between enterprises were fully discussed in the Czechoslovak literature during the debate on economic reform (Šik [1968]). It was stressed that, as in the case of conflicts of interest within an enterprise, the relative shortage in the supply of consumer goods and of individual and social services, which in the existing stage of development of the economy is inevitable, as making the maximisation of individual incomes the main incentive. This tendency is reinforced by the prevalence of monotonous and arduous forms of work which make it impossible for those engaged in the productive process to find self-expression and job satisfaction.

In the case of an enterprise this situation means that the workers collectively are interested in maximising their material advantage. This inevitably leads to conflicts of interest between supplier and customer enterprises, between agricultural and industrial undertakings, between enterprises producing primary materials and those using such materials. Such conflicts of interest could, in the view of the Czechoslovak reformers, be more easily reduced if enterprises gave expression to their diverging interests through direct contacts between themselves, while compulsory central planning as practised hitherto was removed. Within an overall planning framework horizontal relationships between individual enterprises would arise which would be similar to market relationships. It was important to prevent enterprises from obtaining advantages at the expense of others or other groups in society without rendering an appropriate counter-service. Open and publicly-controlled policies for incomes, taxation, investment and social services were required for this task, which might in exceptional cases be of a compulsory character.

The conflict between enterprise and society needs to be more concretely described. The interests of the enterprise can be interpreted as the group interest of the collectivity of workers. The 'interest of society' manifests itself in various more or less general common concerns extraneous to the enterprise. One could exemplify such social concerns through slogans such as 'individual consumption', 'the social wage', 'environment', 'balance between regions', 'education'. All these examples of the common interest, and many others could be mentioned, should make it clear that over and above the particular interests of producers of goods and services, there are common concerns of society. It would be the function of the system as a whole to bring the partial interests as far as possible into harmony with the social interests. In specific instances the worker himself is in an ambivalent interest situation, for example in the case of environmental pollution and certain types of consumer goods production. The conflict of interests here discussed, enterprise versus society, which is conditioned by the relative scarcity of resources, should not be confused with the basic conflict of interests formulated earlier between élites and rank-and-file-worker, even though there are interrelationships between the two types of conflict. The objective contradiction between particular and common interest caused by the basic condition of resource scarcity would, according to the Czechoslovak reform model, be solved by a rational synthesis of central and decentralised planning.

3.4 Participation and the degree of centralisation of the planning process

The degree of centralisation in the planning system which results from the relationship between central and decentralised decision-making is of prime importance for the question of participation of workers in decision-making. The greater the degree of centralisation in planning, in other words the greater the number of centralised planning decisions, the greater is the danger that the contradiction between the central planning bureaucracy on the one hand and the workers in enterprises on the other becomes rigidly established.

Another argument against too high a degree of centralised planning is the fact that the participation of the population in decisions at the central level is much more difficult to organise than the participation of workers in decisions at the enterprise level. This, in turn, is due to the fact that the problems which have to be solved at the central level and which affect the whole of society are altogether more complex, more subtle and less predictable in their results than the problems that have to be decided at plant level. It is well known that for similar reasons methods of participation at the immediate place of work are much easier to organise than participation at the level of the enterprise as a whole. There are limits to the capacity of organs involved in a system of participatory planning to absorb information. The chance to make such participatory planning a reality therefore rises with the degree of decentralisation in the system.

This is not the place to discuss the various concepts of decentralisation in Eastern Europe in detail. It was the generally accepted thesis of the reformers that a synthesis of centralised and decentralised decision-making in planning could best ensure the harmonisation of individual, collective and societal interests. We would now like to indicate on the basis of the Czechoslovak reform model which economically relevant matters are best decided at the central and which at the decentralised level (Kosta [1973]).

There is a series of economic decisions for which, in the view of the reformers, planning at the centralised level is most appropriate. These are planning decisions on macro-structural development including the key investment decisions which determine the structure, such as the determination of the most important proportions between different branches of the economy, the proportions between consumption and investment, the relationship of collective and personal consumption, the structure of regional development, the development of exports (this perhaps to be laid down according to key products and regions), the most important development of the social and cultural infrastructure (health, social security, education, science, housing, etc.), of the technical infrastructure (transport, communications, research and major projects), and finally the establishment of an 'indirect' system of framework planning and guidance for economic and social policy.

Matters which can suitably be the subject of primarily decentralised decision-making by plants and individuals within the framework of central economic policy directives include: individual choices about consumption and employment, the assortment of goods at enterprise level, the specification of basic materials and investment of goods within the framework of a more general plan at the level of industry. Individual services like repair workshops, etc., retail trade organisations, restaurants and hotels, travel bureaux, etc., should also be within the realm of decentralised decision-making.

The following criteria are, in our opinion, crucial for determining the limits between central and decentralised decision-making:

(i) Criteria relating to production-costs, duration of the investment process and of cash flow. If production costs are very high (e.g. nuclear power stations), if the process of capital investment is very long (e.g. computers, including research and development), if there is a long time-interval before invested capital brings a return (e.g. purchase of aircraft) – in such cases centralised rather than de-centralised planning decisions are appropriate.

(ii) Criteria relating to consumption[8] – social as against individual consumption, non-economic considerations.

Decisions about specific public requirements (e.g. building of parks) are decided at central level. Decisions about individual requirements according to the exclusion principle, that is the exclusion of consumers who are not prepared to acquire consumer goods for payment, are decided at decentralised level. Non-economic considerations (e.g. social or cultural or similar matters), 'satisfaction' of 'meritorious needs' (e.g. housing subsidies, free textbooks), can be cited as reasons for the use of central planning intervention.

If the socialist planned economy is to be based on central as well as decentralised decisions then participation is necessary at both levels. Any attempt to introduce a participatory system at the plant level without smashing the structure of administrative bureaucratic decision-making at the centre would be condemned to failure from the start. Participatory organs in plants such as workers' councils would degenerate to mere administrative organs in the strait-jacket of centralised directives. The same would presumably be true for any attempt to introduce participation in the economic system while an authoritarian bureaucratic political system survived.

It would go beyond the scope of this essay to discuss the problems of participation in central planning decisions, which were debated in the Prague Spring but which could not be tried out in practice. Following our analysis of the institutional forms of participation at the decentralised level, especially of the workers' councils, we would now venture some concluding remarks on the interrelationship between the institution of workers' councils and the economic reform model as exemplified by the Czechoslovak experience.

3.5 Workers' Councils and the Economic System

If we assume that the workers' councils of the Prague Spring became in practice, but contrary to the official guidelines, the policy-making bodies within enterprises, the question arises how much freedom of decision the economic reform model left to these councils. It has to be noted that the use and the combination of the factors of production, the long-term production programme, as well as the organisational forms of the enterprise were not determined through central commands, targets or similar obligatory directives from above but were left, within the framework of indirect economic policy directives, to the decision-makers within enterprises. The range of indirect instruments of economic policy corresponded to the criteria of the market: prices, costs, profits. It has to be stressed, however, and the term 'regulated market mechanism' indicates as much, that the intensity of central intervention was much higher than is the case in Western market economies and that in consequence, and also as a result of the abolition of private ownership of the means of production and of the returns on private capital connected with it, important elements of the traditional market system of the West were missing (Kosta [1973]). This is reinforced by the fact that the income of workers and employees was only in small measure dependent on the profits of the enterprise (profit-sharing)—so about 2–3 per cent of the total income (Kosta [1973]) – so that the Czechoslovak model was in this respect essentially different from the system of workers' self-management practised in Yugoslavia.

If we take into account this relationship of plant participation with macro-economic mechanisms of co-ordination, then the claim seems to us justified that the workers' councils and with them the managers of enterprises were left a sufficiently autonomous sphere of decision-making. At the same time this system, at least in its abstract form, contained an adequate measure of regulative and control devices to obviate the danger of anarchy in the economic process.

Amongst the most important conditions of successful participation at plant level is the need, as the Yugoslav example shows, for an adequate data base for the workers' councils, and for their collective organs. To obtain the necessary capacity to absorb and process information, it is necessary to ensure a sufficient level of qualification amongst members. For this purpose a process of theoretical and practical training has to be permanently provided; additionally the self-administering unit must be of limited size; in other words there must be a favourable relationship between the number of workers' representatives and the number of workers represented by them. The first of these preconditions, a high level of education, was largely met in Czechoslovakia but the second, smaller self-governing units, would have needed, as was mentioned earlier, further action.

The Czechoslovak workers' councils of 1968 and 1969 provided an experience which in spite of all problems and weaknesses and the short-lived nature of the experiment will presumably influence all future attempts to establish a system of participation within socialist planned economies.

NOTES

1. The major portion of this section and parts also of Sections 2.1 and 3.2 are taken from the text of a lecture delivered by the author at a conference of French Socialists in Paris in November 1972 on the subject of 'Czechoslovakia, Socialism and Democracy'. The lecture was published under the title 'Socialism and Self Government' in *Wiener Tagebuch* (1973). Cf. also Kosta [1974] and [1975].
2. The most important sections in German in Borin and Plogen [1970] pp. 74–88.
3. The figures given in this Section are based on the study by Pravda referred to above (Pravda [1975] p. 9, Kosta [1973]).
4. *Reporter*, No. 16 (1969).
5. See note 1 above. Cf. Svejnar [1974].
6. See note 1 above.
7. Cf. amongst others, Deutscher [1967] pp. 38–40, Gorz [1967]and Šik [1976].

8. The distinguishing factors between centralised and decentralised planning which are here called 'criteria based on consumption' are broadly equivalent to the distinction made by Musgrave between centralised budget financing and decentralised financing mechanisms based on the market: cf. Musgrave [1969].

REFERENCES

Borin, Max, and Plogen, Vera [1970], *Management und Selbstverwaltung in der CSSR* [Management and Self-Government in Czechoslovakia] (Rotbuch 4, West Berlin) pp. 74–88.

Deutscher, Issac [1967], *Die unvollendete Revolution 1917–1967* [The Incomplete Revolution 1917–1967] (Frankfurt) pp. 38–40, 40–9.

Fišera, Josef and Vladimir [1970], 'Die tschechoslowakischen Arbeiterrate' [The Czechoslovak Workers' Councils], *Wiener Tagebuch* [Vienna Diary], 9.

Gorz, André [1967], Der Schwierige Sozialismus [Difficult Socialism] (Frankfurt) pp. 117–18.

Kosta, Jiři [1973], 'Sozialismus and Selbstverwaltung' [Socialism and Self-Government], *Wiener Tagebuch*, 2, p. 21.

Kosta, Jiři [1973], 'The Main Features of the Czechoslovak Economic Reform, in *The Czechoslovak Reform Movement 1968*, V. V. Kusin (ed.), p. 138. (German version, 'Die tschechoslowakische Wirtschaftsreform der sechziger Jahre', in *Sozialistische Marktwirtschaften*, H. Leipold (ed.) (Munich, 1975) pp. 53, 57.)

Kosta, Jiři [1974], *Sozialistische Planwirtschaft* [The Socialist Planned Economy] (Opladen) pp. 188–92, 199–202.

Kosta, Jiři [1975], 'Betriebliche Selbstverwaltung und sozialistische Planwirtschaft' [Self-Government in Enterprises and Socialist Planning], in *Systemwandel und Demokratisierung* [System Change and Democratisation] (Koln) pp. 162–8.

Musgrave, Richard A. [1968], *Finanztheorie* [Financial Theory] (German version, Tübingen) pp. 6–19.

Pravda, Alex [1975], 'Workers' Participation in Czechoslovakia 1968–1969', paper delivered at the annual conference of NASEES, London, pp. 1–5, 9, 12–15, 16, 17–21.

Rudé Právo, [1968], Akění program KSČ [Action Programme of the Czech Communist Party], p. 297f.

Šik, Ota [1968], *Plán a trh za socialismu* [Plan and Market under Socialism] (Prague) Section II-2-c. (German version, Plan und Markt in Sozialismus (Vienna, 1967).)

Šik, Ota [1976], Das kommunistische Machsystem [The Communist System of Power] (Hamburg) pp. 28–38.

Švejnar, Jan [1974]. 'Czechoslovakian Labor Relations: The Postwar Experience' (Part II: 'From the Prague Spring to the Present Day'), *Forum* (Cornell University) pp. 128–31.

6 Institutional Forms of Worker Participation in the Federal German Republic

Z. Almanasreh

PREFATORY REMARKS

This paper investigates briefly how far the institutional framework established in the Federal German Republic after the Second World War facilitates meaningful participation in decision-making by workers and employees. In addition the consequences for the stability of the total system will be briefly sketched.

Within the scope of this chapter, it is not possible to give a full definition of the meaning of participation in general and of participation by workers and employees in particular. We take as our starting-point the demands of the organised representatives of workers and employees in the Federal Republic as they are to be found in the programmes of the trade unions. The purpose of our inquiry is to what extent the institutional framework helps to fulfil these requirements though this does not exclude a few remarks which go beyond this purpose. In order to put developments into perspective the first part of the essay contains a short description of the position in the immediate post-war years 1945–9. In the second part, the legal basis for the three essential areas of participation for workers and employees are briefly surveyed: 1. the Wage Contract Law; 2. the Works Constitution Act; and 3. the Law on Co-determination. This is followed by a discussion of the proposals currently being debated for further developing co-determination. There follows in the third part a critical analysis of the results which could be achieved and to some extent have already been achieved on the basis of the present laws.

HISTORICAL STARTING-POINT, 1945–9

The almost total collapse of the German economy in the Second World

War produced a situation in which the primary necessities of life and employment could no longer be guaranteed. In these circumstances the main task of officials in plants and local trade unions was the provision of food, fuel and shelter and to get production going again, in many cases before the owners of factories reappeared (Bergmann [1975] p. 122, and Schmidt [1972] p. 13). The activities of trade unions were concentrated in accordance with the wishes of the Allies at the level of the plant and locality. The occupying powers did not initially tolerate links above the regional level.

In view of this attitude of the Allies confining them to local and specific activities, the trade unions had to give up their original intention to create a single, centrally-directed trade union. Instead they formed an association of autonomous industrial unions (Bergmann [1975] p. 123, Schmidt [1972] p. 14 ff., and Zink [1957] p. 281 ff.).

The long-term aims of the unions for reform were still marked by the ideas of economic democracy current in the Weimar period. They wanted a new economic order with trade union participation ('Die Gewerksschaftsbewegung . . .' [1949] p. 79 ff.), but they put their trust in a parliamentary realisation of such aims, especially as all parties at this time had more or less similar ideas for a new economic order in their programmes. Above the plant and enterprise level the trade unions demanded the socialisation of key industries and of the big banks. The unions wanted equality of representation in the process of 'state economic planning' and in the various organs of economic self-government. At the level of the plant, they wanted far-reaching regulations for co-determination providing for parity in the composition of supervisory boards of all major enterprises and the right of control by works councils of all economic, social and personnel matters. The 'Munich Programme', passed at the foundation congress of the DGB in 1949, treats economic planning, common ownership and co-determination as a unity. Only taken together will they constitute a new economic order based on full employment, prosperity for all and social justice. (Cf. Bergmann [1975] document 13, p. 125.)

The unions hoped to gain the support of the Allies for their demands for a new economic order. They put their trust in the political parties and assumed that the experiences of the Nazi period and the new economic and political circumstances were creating, for the first time, the possibility of a democratic economic order. These hopes were soon to be disappointed. Under the lead of the United States the Allies prevented, through the conditions of the Marshall Plan and through direct intervention, any measure which could have favoured the establishment of a non-capitalist new order.

The western Allies, especially the Americans, were determined to permit in West Germany only an economic order which was favourable to their interests. These interests were defined by the necessities of the Cold War. The guideline of this policy was the concept of West Germany as a capitalist bulwark against communism. Therefore no socialist experiments of any type were to be permitted. (Schmidt [1972] p. 25).

The military government was in a position to suspend the socialisation laws in Northrhine-Westphalia, decided upon by due democratic process. The decrees for socialisation in Hesse were rendered ineffective when the military government by special decree exempted the most important enterprises from these measures (Clay [1950] pp. 327 and 357). The threat of resistance from the trade unions was ignored.

Schmidt reaches the following conclusion:

> By the time the Federal Republic was founded, little was left of the efforts of the trade unions to establish a new economic order after the collapse of the Third Reich: there was the co-determination law, limited to the coal and steel industries, and a series of legal enactments which had mostly been suspended (Schmidt [1972] p. 27).

On the other hand the restoration of an economy based on private capital was proceeding apace in connection with the Marshall Plan. The economic council in the bi-zone was able, with the support of the Allies and free of trade union influence, to proceed towards the establishment of a market economy. The economic situation in the western zones was rapidly stabilised and the trade unions, which contributed to this rapid stabilisation by their restraint in wage demands, were now pushed into the role of an opposition operating within the system. The American economist Wallich comments:

> The most important contribution of trade union policy on wages was towards financing investment. The fact that wages lagged behind prices created high profits which enabled industry to finance itself in large measure. Unequal distribution of income, favouring the higher income groups with their greater rate of saving, was an essential factor in the growth of investment . . . . In December 1948, six months after the currency reform, the index of industrial prices stood at 192 (1938 = 100) while hourly wages were moving around 143. The index figures for raw materials and capital goods stood at 195. In this gap lay the origins of an exceptional rate of profit and ability of self-financing. These optimistic expectations in turn added to the incentive to invest (Wallich [1955] p. 281 ff.).

The basic programme adopted by the German trade union federation in 1949 still contains demands for co-determination, common ownership of the means of production, and direction of the economy according to 'the principles of full employment and to each according to his needs' – demands therefore for a fundamental change in the economic system. By the time the pragmatically-orientated economic policy of the German trade unions of the DGB was promulgated on 12 March 1951, these demands had been blocked. The trade unions unequivocally accepted the social market economy and only asked for measures to improve the system in the interests of the workers (Schmidt [1972] p. 37). A paragraph of the proceedings of the DGB 1950–51 dealing with the question 'free market economy or planning' shows clearly the readiness of the trade union leadership to become integrated:

'The attitude of the trade unions to the question of a planned or free market economy is in no way dogmatic. They do not favour or reject in principle either the release of entrepreneurial forces or their absolute control. They are of the opinion that, as in all matters affecting society, a reasonable degree of freedom should be allowed ('Geschaftsbericht des DGB' [1950/51] p. 231).

On the one hand Erhard and Adenauer were intensively and successfully engaged in establishing a system of private enterprise with social obligations (social market economy); while on the other hand the confused demands of the trade unions 'that economic considerations should be tempered by social ones, that the economic principle should be accompanied by the social principle' ('Geschaftsbericht des DGB' [1950/51]) found no expression in a concrete alternative political concept.

The legal basis for the participation of workers and employees described below must be seen against this background and within the framework of the newly established system of a market economy in the Federal Republic. The co-determination rights of the trade unions as representatives of workers in the Federal German Republic are based essentially on the collective agreement Law of 25 August 1969, on the Works Constitution Act of 15 January 1972, and on the law about the co-determination of workers and employees on the boards of enterprises in the mining industry and in the iron and steel industry, in its changed form of 6 September 1965.

THE LEGAL BASIS OF PARTICIPATION

The Wage Contract Law

These comments are, unless otherwise stated, based on the Wage Contract Law (TVG) – Tarifvertragsgesetz) in the version published on 25 August 1969 (BGB [German Civil Code] I.p. 1323), published in Beck-Texte [1974].

The relationship of partners to wage agreements whose free bargaining rights are guaranteed by the constitution of the Federal Republic are regulated by the Wage Contract Law in a form that is only very general and requires interpretation. Detailed regulations on the rights and obligations of partners to wage agreements are defined by the Courts and through generally recognised usages. According to the law 'partners in wage negotiations' are empowered to conclude wage contracts: 'The wage contract regulates the rights and obligations of the parties to the wage contract and contains regulatory norms for ordering the content and the ending of conditions of employment as well as of questions concerning the enterprise and the constitution of the enterprise.' Parties to wage agreements can be trade unions or individual employees as well as associations of employers and federation of employers (national organisations) empowered to conclude agreements. Wage contracts are binding on all individual members of partners to such agreements. If they are declared generally binding such agreements affect all employers and employees in the area for which they are valid. The wage contract can be declared generally binding by the Federal Minister for Employment and Social Order at the request of one of the partners to the wage agreement. The areas for which wage contracts are valid are determined by considerations of subject, locality and personnel. There is no general principle determining the validity of contracts. If, for example, a contract is valid for a particular industry, this can mean a multiplicity of branches of an industry, such as the whole metal industry with millions of employees, but it can also mean narrowly defined small branches, for instance in the food industry, with only a few hundred employees.

As for locality, the whole area of the Federal Republic is divided into numerous wage districts, which do not necessarily coincide with the Länder or other administrative boundaries, and for which the so-called regional wage contract is valid.

As for personnel, wage contracts may often make a distinction between workers and white-collar employees.

Among the subjects dealt with by wage contracts are hours, overtime rates, payment for danger and hardship, Sunday, holiday and night work, leave, and, within the wage and salary scales, the groups, the definition of groups, job definition, age relationships. More recently questions of capital distribution have been dealt with in the wage negotiations. In addition to wage contracts, there are often separate agreements about hours, holidays and compensation for redundancy (Politik und Programm [1974] p. 178).

Wage agreements are fixed through 'wage negotiations'. In case of conflict, when no agreement is possible, arbitration by neutral bodies is invoked. If neither of these methods produces agreement, then as a last resort industrial action (strikes) to enforce trade union demands are possible. If industrial action is to be within the law, it must satisfy certain conditions. It must not infringe the obligation of the bargaining partners to reach a peaceful settlement. A strike threat or a ballot concerning it are not legal while a wage contract is in force or negotiations are in progress, or until arbitration procedures have been exhausted. A principle of social equivalence must be observed in industrial conflicts. A strike can only be declared against the partner to a wage contract and only a party to a wage contract can call a strike. If one of these principles is infringed, the strike can be declared illegal and become a wildcat strike. Industrial action is required to be fair. Good behaviour is to be observed. For the employer, the lockout is the action equivalent to a strike.

These are the general legal regulations affecting free wage bargaining. The extent to which this general formal framework is in practice observed or exhausted by the parties to a wage contract depends on the general economic and political conditions and cannot be taken for granted. We will return to this question below.

Works Constitution Act (BVG)

The Act of 15 January 1972 provides for the establishment of works councils in enterprises, with the rule that it is possible to establish at least five permanent employees entitled to vote, of whom three are to be elected. For a company in which there are several works councils, there must also be a works council for the whole company. For a combine there must be a works council for the whole combine. The function of trade unions and of employers' associations, 'especially the representation of the interests of their members', as well as valid wage agreements, are not affected by this law. Trade unions and employers' associations should have full access to an enterprise. 'Employers and works councils collaborate in mutual trust for the benefit of employees and of the enterprise, observing wage agreements which are in force, and in co-operation with the trade unions and employers' associations represented in the enterprise.'

The law distinguishes between workers, salaried employees and managers. The BVG does not apply to the latter. The works council is chosen in direct elections. Entitled to vote are all employees who have reached their eighteenth birthday. Eligible are all those entitled to vote who have been in the firm at least six months, or who as domestic workers have worked mainly for the firm. The number of members on the works council is determined by the size of the firm and ranges from one member in firms of five employees to 31 in enterprises of 9000 employees.

The works council is normally elected every three years in the period between 1 March and 31 May and seats on the council are distributed between the representatives of workers and salaried employees according to the proportion of these two groups in the firm. As far as possible the works council should be composed of employees from the various sub-departments and dependent enterprises and the sexes should be represented according to their numerical strength in the enterprise. The period of office of the works council is three years. Members of the works council are protected against dismissal and professional disadvantage for the duration of their membership. Membership ceases at the end of the period of office, upon resignation or loss of eligibility through legal decision or exclusion from the works council. A number of works council members determined by the size of the enterprise have the right to be released from their normal work duties. The works council elects a chairman who conducts negotiations with the employer within the decisions taken by the works council. If the works council consists of nine or more members, then an executive committee can be formed which consists of the chairman of the works council, his deputy and other members of the executive committee whose number is determined by the size of the works council. The executive committee so formed conducts the day-to-day business of the works council.

The meetings of the works council are called by the chairman. He lays down the agenda, conducts negotiations and has to summon the members, and where necessary the trustees of handicapped workers and young workers' delegates, to meetings, giving due notice. Meetings of works councils are held during working hours and are not open to the public.

The works council has to call a General Meeting of employees of the enterprise once every calendar year, at which a report has to be rendered. The employer must be invited to this meeting and is entitled to address it. The employer is obliged, once every year, to make a report to the general meeting 'about the personnel and social arrangements of the enterprise' and 'about the economic position and development of the enterprise', 'provided industrial and commercial secrets are not endangered'.

The works council is obliged to summon the works General Meeting if the employer, or at least a quarter of the employees who have the right to vote, ask for it.

The Works General Meeting 'can deal with matters affecting the enterprise and its employees, including those concerned with wages policy, social policy and economic questions'.

The works constitution law contains detailed principles which regulate the form and the content of the collaboration between the works council, as the autonomous representative of the employees at the level of the plant, and the employer. A formal framework is thus established for the collaboration and co-determination of the employees.

General Principles of Collaboration

(i) Employer and works council must negotiate on matters of dispute with the serious intent to reach agreement and must put forward proposals for the settlement of differences of opinion.

(ii) Acts of industrial conflict are not admissible between employer and works council. Employer and works council have to refrain from actions which could damage the process of production or the tranquillity of the enterprise. They have to refrain from any party political activity within the enterprise.

(iii) For the settlement of differences of opinion a conciliation committee is to be formed. This has to consist of an equal number of assessors appointed by the works council and by the employer and an impartial chairman on whose appointment both sides have to reach agreement. If there is failure to agree on the number of assessors or the appointment of the chairman, a decision of the labour court is required. The conciliation committee reaches its decisions by majority vote, 'having due regard to the interests of the enterprise and of the employees affected'.

(iv) If the intervention of the conciliation committee does not produce agreement, then either of the parties can take action in the labour court, whose decisions are binding.

(v) Agreements between the works council and the employer are put into effect by the employer. They are 'mandatory and directly applicable' but can be, unless otherwise agreed, terminated at three months' notice.

(vi) The members of the works council, or of other bodies representing employees on the basis of the Works Constitution Act, may not be obstructed or disturbed in the execution of their duties. The members of the works council are obliged not to reveal or to make use of industrial and commercial secrets expressly designated by the employer as requiring secrecy.

(vii) The works council has the following functions:

(*a*) to supervise the execution of all laws, regulations, measures for the prevention of accidents, wage agreements and general agreements made to protect the interests of the employees;

(*b*) to require the employer to take such measures as are in the interests of the enterprise and its employees;

(*c*) to receive suggestions from employees and young workers' delegates and, in so far as they seem useful, to ensure that they are put into effect through negotiation with the employer;

(*d*) to facilitate the employment of handicapped persons and others in need of special protection;

(*e*) to prepare and arrange the election of young workers' delegates and to collaborate with them in the interests of young workers;

(*f*) to help the employment of older employees in the enterprise;

(*g*) to ensure the integration of foreign workers in the enterprise and to advance the understanding between them and German employees.

Employees' rights of participation and complaint
(i) The employer is obliged to inform the employee about his place of work, his tasks and responsibilities as well as about the nature of his work and about changes in his field of work.
(ii) The employee has the right to be heard on all measures taken by the employer which concern him. He can demand that the calculation and composition of his remuneration and his prospects of career development should be explained to him. He can also ask to be shown his personal file and to have it commented upon.
(iii) The employee has the right of complaint and the right to receive a reply to his complaint without suffering any personal detriment.

Co-determination rights of the works council
The works council has, in the absence of legislation or a collective agreement, to participate in determining the following matters:
(*a*) Social matters: this includes questions such as plant regulations, commencement and end of daily working hours, temporary changes in working hours customary in the enterprise, holiday schedules, works studies to measure the output of employees, social provisions, wage scales, piece-work and bonus rates and safety regulations.
(*b*) Conditions affecting the place of work, the process of production and the work environment: if, according to recognised norms of plant management, these conditions run counter to the dignified conduct of work, the works council can demand appropriate measures for the prevention, alleviation or compensation of such shortcomings.
(*c*) Personal questionnaires, principles of evaluation, guidelines on personnel selection in cases of engagement, promotions, redeployments or dismissals, as well as measures affecting individuals.
(*d*) Education and training programmes in the plant.

Information and Consultation rights of the works council
The employer has to give the works council early information on the following:
(*a*) Changes that will affect the place of work and process of production or the work environment;
(*b*) Personnel planning;
(*c*) Professional training of employees;
(*d*) Economic matters – in enterprises with more than 100 permanent employees, an economic committee is to be formed for the discussion of economic matters with the employer and to keep the works council informed of these;
(*e*) Changes in the production process, normally in enterprises with more than 20 employees eligible to vote.

Law on Co-determination of Employees in the Boards and Supervisory Boards of Enterprises in the Mining, Iron and Steel Industries

These comments on the legal basis of co-determination in general enterprises (BVG—Betriebsverfassungsgesetz [The Works Constitution Act]) and in the enterprises of the mining, iron and steel industry (Co-determination Law), are based on the text of the laws as published in Beck-Texte [1974].

The co-determination rights of employees on the supervisory boards, and on bodies charged with their legal representation, cover the following types of enterprise: public companies, limited liability companies and mining companies with independent legal status. They must normally employ more than 1000 employees or be unitary companies (i.e. without subsidiaries) and they must operate in mining or in the iron and steel industries. The extension of co-determination to companies with controlling interests was laid down in the amendment of the Co-determination Law of 6 September 1965.

Members of the Supervisory Board and their Election
The supervisory board consists of :
(*a*) four representatives of the shareholders and one further member;
(*b*) four representatives of the employees and a further member, of whom one worker and one employee have to be drawn from the enterprise and two members have to be nominated for election by the trade unions represented in the enterprise; and
(*c*) one additional member.
The additional members may not in any way be dependent upon the enterprise, the trade unions or the employer organisations.

In companies with a nominal capital of more than DM 20,000,000 the board can consist of 15 members; and in companies with a nominal capital of more than DM 50,000,000, of 21 members. The principle of parity in the composition of supervisory boards has to be observed throughout. The number of workers belonging to the enterprise rises to two and of those nominated by the trade unions to three in the first case; and to three and four respectively in the second.

All representatives of the employees are elected by the electoral college, which is the general assembly of the company. Nominations of the trade unions and of the works council are, however, binding. The eleventh 'neutral member' is also chosen by the electoral college on the basis of a majority nomination by the elected members of the board.

The supervisory board appoints the members of the organ which is the legal representative of the company (the board of management). A workers' director is appointed as an equal member of the board of management and his appointment cannot be made against the vote of a majority of the representatives of the employees on the supervisory board. 'Normally the workers' director is particularly responsible for personnel and social questions' (Beck-Texte [1974] p. 299).

Extended co-determination proposals currently under discussion

The extension of co-determination by employees at the level of the enterprise is advocated more or less by all political parties. There are, however, still differing views about the form of future legislation and the most important proposals are briefly described here.

Demands of the Trade Unions

Cf. the DGB proposal for a 'Law on Co-determination for Employees in Major Enterprises and Corporations', published in March 1968.

The trade unions support the model of co-determination in the coal and steel industries described earlier, the core of which is parity of representation on the supervisory board. This would offer a suitable basis for qualified co-determination, leading to parity of labour and capital, which in turn could produce a change in the distribution of power in favour of workers, provided the representatives of the workers know how to use the instrument of co-determination in an enterprise and provided there is a close link with the trade unions as well as with the institutions of co-determination in the plant and at the company level. The trade unions therefore demand the extension of this model of co-determination to all private and public undertakings as well as the realisation of co-determination at a level above the enterprise (at the level of the whole economy).

According to the proposals of the DGB, co-determination should be extended to all companies which are in the form of a public company and which have two of the following characteristics: 2000 employees, profits of DM75,000,000, or a turnover of DM150,000,000. With banks the criterion should be, instead of size of turnover, the total sum of payments made for the business transacted by the bank; and with insurance companies the gross amount of premium income. The exclusion of certain types of personal company is in the view of the DGB only a practical question, not a matter of principle.

The trade unions also demand co-determination on the basis of parity in the federal economic and social council, in the social and economic councils of the Länder and in the regional social and economic councils. Trade union federations at the various levels should be entitled to send representatives.

CDU Proposals

Cf. on this and the SPD and FDP proposals: Economic Council of the CDU [1973].

The CDU proposals provide for a slight preponderance of the shareholding side because the principle of parity is seen as difficult to operate in practice. On the supervisory board there should be seven representatives of the shareholders and five representatives of the employees. Representatives of the employees would be elected by the whole workforce. A majority of these representatives would have to be employed within the enterprise. The employees would have the right to be represented on the board of directors and in the committees of the board. If a proposal were to be out-voted by a unanimous vote of the shareholders, then there would be an obligation to provide a reasoned justification. Publicity on matters in dispute would be permissible in plant and enterprise.

Managing executives would have an active and passive right of election on the side of the employees and would be represented by their own committee of spokesmen.

The trade unions represented within the enterprise would have the right to nominate one or two representatives of the employees. The representatives of the employees would have the right to take part in the procedure for appointing members of the board of management 'at the stage of pre-selection'. One member of the board of management must be responsible for personnel and social matters.

Regular reporting about social provision is obligatory. These co-determination regulations should apply to public companies, joint stock companies with upwards of 2000 employees, family companies in the form of shareholding companies with upwards of 500 employees, limited liability companies, limited partnerships with a company as general partner, mining works with separate legal status, insurance companies and co-operatives with upwards of 500 workers.

The CDU rejects co-determination on the basis of parity as incompatible with the social market economy. The claim of trade unions to act as representatives is also rejected as incompatible with the principle of full trusteeship.

The SPD proposals

The SPD demand in their proposals full parity in co-determination and differ from the DGB in essentials only on the following points:
(i) The DGB demands that the workers' representatives from outside the enterprise should be delegated by the trade unions. Against this the SPD suggests that such representatives should be nominated for election after consultation with the works councils but that this pre-selection should be binding on the electoral college.
(ii) The SPD demands that one member of the board of management, which is to consist of at least three, should be predominantly responsible for personnel and social matters; but there are no special suggestions about how this member is to be appointed. In the DGB proposals there

must be one of the workers' directors who cannot be chosen against a majority vote of the workers' representatives and who must act as an equal member of the board of management responsible for personnel and social matters.

(iii) In the SPD proposals, the electoral college of the workers representatives is the general assembly of the enterprise, whereas in the DGB proposals it is the general meeting of all the works councils.

The FDP proposals

The FDP demands juridical and arithmetical parity. A stalemate situation, it says, has positive value in bringing about the highest compulsion towards agreement. Managing executives would, however, be included on the employees' side: they would elect two out of six workers' representatives on the supervisory board on the nomination of a committee of managing executives. Eligible would be 'only such managing employees who, below the level of the directorate of the enterprise and its extensions, exercise directing functions as well as employee function'. (See Economic Council of the CDU [1973] p. 18.) The remaining four representatives of the employees must be working within the enterprise and would be elected by the total workforce.

The chairman of the supervisory board would have to be elected in principle by a two-thirds majority of members of the board. If there were no majority, then the chairman would be appointed alternately from the representatives of the workers and those of the shareholders.

The trade unions would not have the right either to delegate or to propose representatives.

One member of the board of directors would have to be responsible for personnel and social matters. His appointment, however, would be made in the same way as that of other members. Co-determination should extend to all companies, including limited liability companies and limited partnerships with a company as general partner, having 1500 employees upwards. The co-determination model existing in the coal, iron and steel industries is rejected.

Co-determination model of the coalition parties, SPD and FDP

Comments on these proposals are taken from the *Frankfurter Allgemeine Zeitung (FAZ)* [1974].

The basis of these proposals is a supervisory board of 20 members; for smaller enterprises the number could be reduced to 14 or 10.

Ten members would represent the shareholders or owners and ten the employees. The workers' representatives would consist of seven people employed in the plants of the enterprise and taken from the three groups of employees in their due proportion, and three representatives of the trade unions represented in the plants. The chairman of the supervisory board would be elected for the period of office of the board by a two-thirds majority of board members from among the representatives of the shareholders or owners; but his deputy would be elected from among the representatives of the employees. If there were no two-thirds majority, the chairman and his deputy would change places annually between the two groups.

In a stalemate situation a second vote would be taken in which the chairman would have a casting vote if a majority of each of the two groups so agreed.

Representatives of the employees would be chosen by electors. The number of electors would be determined by a key number which would allow each of the three groups, workers, salaried employees and executives, to be represented according to their strength in the enterprise. One-tenth of each group would have the right to nominate.

The electoral college of the enterprise would consist of the chosen electors who elect the seven employees' representatives belonging to the enterprise. The three representatives of the trade unions would also be chosen by the electoral college. The nominations of the trade unions represented in the enterprise would, however, be binding. The representatives of the shareholders or owners are chosen by the general meeting.

The members of the board of management would be chosen by simple majority by the supervisory board. They would all have equal rights and one of them must be responsible for personnel matters and social provisions.

These co-determination regulations are applicable to all enterprises which have the legal form of a public company. a limited partnership, a company with limited liability, an enterpree in the mining industry with independent legal status, an insurance company based on mutuality, a commercial or production co-operative or a limited partnership with a company as general partner and which employs more than 2000 employees, as well as for leading subsidiaries within comberes which come under the co-determination regulations.

Co-determination in the coal and steel industry, as well as co-determination under the Works Constitution Law in the remaining areas will not be affected.

Policy and practice of the trade unions
Since the efforts of the trade unions to obtain fundamental changes in the economic order proved abortive in the immediate post-war years, the unions confined themselves thereafter to wage and social policy. In this area, there was need to make up much lost ground owing to the restraint which the unions had exercised in the difficult economic conditions during the rebuilding of the economy.

The guiding concept in the wage policy of the unions during this phase was described by the then director of the Economic Institute of the Trade

Unions (WWI), Victor Agartz, as in general terms 'an expansive wages policy'. He had developed his basic ideas on this subject as early as 1950. In his address at the Frankfurt Federal Congress of the DGB, at the end of 1953, he gave concrete expression to his concept of an expansive wages policy. This comprised three ideas: a wages policy which is active, dynamic and expansive in a narrower sense (Bergmann (1975) p. 157). Agartz declared at the Congress that

> since 1952 wages and salaries had followed the development of prices and of production only cautiously, without exhausting all the possibilities and without correcting the disproportion between wages and prices. The workforce had shown, in the years since the currency reform, a self-discipline, particularly in matters of wages, which had earned it as little gratitude as a similar gigantic achievement in the years after the stabilisation of the Mark in 1924 (Protokoll des 3 ord. Bundeskongresses des DGB [Protocol of the Third Ordinary Congress of the DGB], Frankfurt 1954, p. 455, quoted in Schmidt [1972] p. 49).

From the start the trade unions justified an expansive wage policy by reasoning from within the system. 'Wages in a capitalist economy were always a political reward'; and 'the pursuit of class and group interests in capitalism was the rule.' Consequently the trade unions had to preserve the material interests of their members by an active wages policy. To justify a dynamic wages policy the argument was used that to maintain a high level of economic activity required the maintenance of purchasing power. Since capitalist economies were liable to over-production, a dynamic wages policy would force a constant rise in real wages and thereby in consumer demand so that the economy would remain in balance. According to Agartz, this 'expansive' wages policy is 'the most effective way to force enterprises into constant rationalisation, to maximise productivity and thus to create a firm basis for wage expansion' (Agartz [1953] p. 246). Not only were these arguments based on an acceptance of the existing economic system, the means adopted to pursue these aims were also based on conformity within the system. The arguments were presented as conforming to the existing system, but closer analysis shows all three of them as being in contradiction to a free market economy and so scarcely tenable. The realisation of a dynamic wages policy would probably produce progressive inflation or stagnation and unemployment, since employers would not accept a reduction of profits. The room for manoeuvre which the system allowed was not even fully exploited. In most cases the trade unions were content with negotiation and arbitration. Strikes were rarely resorted to, even when a majority of members were prepared to undertake them. (Cf. Schmidt [1972] p. 48, and Table I on strikes in the Appendix.)

The concept of the 'expansive wages policy' was later replaced by an 'active wages policy'. In its action programme published on 1 May 1955, the DGB adopted for its affiliated unions 'an active policy on wages and salaries', the analytical basis as well as political economic aims of which have not been explicitly explained and justified by the unions to this day. The rare and usually vague explanations of an active wages policy lead to the conclusion that this policy was an important step in the transition from a radical trade union reform programme towards a moderate policy of reform (Bergmann [1975] p. 160).

The aim of maximising the share of wages in the social product is now replaced by the demand for a 'just share' or a just division of the social product. 'Behind our demands for wages and salaries, there is, within the framework of an active wages policy, the aim of a new division of the social product' (Brenner).

The action programme mentioned earlier adds to its demands on wages policy the following requirements of social policy: shortening of hours of work, lengthening of holidays and extension of the system of social security. In this way, wage-earners would obtain a greater share of the general rise in living standards. It can be shown empirically and theoretically that the stated aim is not realised. In so far as the social reforms increase the costs of employers, they are taken into account in wage rises or, if possible, are passed on to the consumer.

The vagueness of the concept of an active wages policy secured for the trade union leaders, who had recognised the limits within which their wages policy would have to operate, the necessary elasticity to hold a balance between the interests of their members and the requirement for stability within the economy.

As time went on, there was an almost complete integration of the wage and salary policy of the trade union with the official policies on incomes and on the economy as a whole. The trade union in the construction industry, IG Bau-Steine-Erden, was the first major German union to accept the formula of a modified wages policy based on productivity which had been recommended by the committee of experts (SVR). The concept of the committee of experts (SVR) of a wages policy neutral in relation to the level of costs follows in broad outline the principles which the trade union of the construction industry had followed even before the setting up of the committee of experts (IG Bau-Steine-Erden, Geschaftsbericht [1966–68] p. 30). The pursuit of a wages policy based on productivity was demanded at the Sixth Annual Conference of the Union by the then Chairman Georg Leber. (Cf. IG Bau-Steine-Erden, Gerwerkschaftstag [1963], Protokoll, p. 234.) The union of the metal industry, IG-Metall, maintained in public the aim of a redistribution of income and rejected wages policy based on productivity, but in practice it could not escape the pressure of economic and political trends.

As they became aware that wages policy in itself would not be effective in redistributing incomes, trade unions incorporated into their ideas on wages a policy on the redistribution of wealth. They developed the idea of capital formation for employees and found a response in various political parties. This demand was not only justified in conformity with the existing economic system but was intended and expressed as a contribution to stabilising the system. The following aims were to be realised: (i) the workers should be given a more just share in the social product; (ii) this share would enable the worker to participate in economic growth and give him an increasing stake as a citizen; (iii) since this planned development of capital formation in the hands of employees does not reduce the amount of investment available for economic growth, a contribution is also made to the stability of the currency. Georg Leber [1964] (pp. 14 and 7), sums up the justification in terms of social policy as follows:

> A distribution of capital and property within a democratic and social framework based on the rule of law would be a true alternative to the collectivist levelling on the other side of the Iron Curtain, where a new order of property distribution brought about a loss of freedom. It shows a lack of political responsibility if we, in the Federal Republic, cannot match this farce of a new property distribution with anything other than a structure of property and capital which still has its roots in the early capitalism of the past two centuries.

With the slogan 'capital formation for the worker' the trade unions also hoped that the changes in the distribution of the social product which could not be obtained by means of a wage and salary policy could now be reached by means of a redistribution of property. But just as the redistribution of the social product in favour of workers is slow to come, so is the redistribution of property. In a study published by the Institute for Social Research, the following conclusions are reached:
(i) All plans for the formation of capital, even those put forward by the trade unions, are concerned only with new capital; the distribution of old capital remains unaffected.
(ii) All the plans so far put forward remain substantially below the 20 per cent limit.
(iii) All schemes for capital formation for workers so far put into practice, be it through trade union wages agreements or through legislative measures or through employers' initiative, have up to now not amounted to more than a modest incentive to saving. In 1971, 14.5 million employees owned an average capital investment of 430 DM. Ten million of these had obtained their investment through wages agreements containing provisions for capital formation. (Cf. Bergmann [1972] p. 167, and for the development of the wage share in the GNP and wealth distribution, Tables II and III in the Appendix.

These amounts devoted to capital formation were treated by the employers as cost factors like wages and were reflected as far as possible in prices.

Large unions like IG-Metall and OTV criticised the policy on capital formation because they regarded it as masking real conflicts. 'This policy cannot fundamentally change the social position of workers, for this type of capital formation cannot free the workers from their dependent position as receivers of wages and salaries. It cannot solve the problem of economic power which arises from the private control of the means of production' (Leitsatze [1972]).

There is a tendency for trade union policy, as here described, to be remote from the shop floor. From some sections of the trade union movement, there are demands for a wages policy controlled by the shop floor and thus giving rank-and-file members more direct representation by strengthening trade union presence and negotiating power in the actual plant. These demands are the result of criticism of existing practices. In fact the demand for a wages policy controlled from the shop floor has been heard only intermittently from the unions, has been strictly rejected by the employers' associations and has not been favourably regarded by the state.

This is all that can be said about the participation of workers through trade union representation in the field of wages policy. At the level of the enterprise and the plant, employees have at their disposal, in form at any rate, other autonomous organs of representation to safeguard their interests but in practice the trade unions play an important role in this area as well. Readiness to accept integration in the system and co-operation with the state, recognisable in trade union practice as here described, is therefore of great importance also in co-determination at the level of the enterprise and the plant.

The investigating commission of the Bundestag reaches the following conclusions from the practice of co-determination in the coal and steel industries. The introduction of co-determination into supervisory boards has produced no changes of policy on the part of enterprises. Boards with equal representation of employers and employees have discharged their control and consultative functions with less conflict and greater efficiency than boards on which the employees are underrepresented; and the presence of internal representatives, as well as those external to the enterprises, has helped the boards to reach decisions more effectively and with less friction. This appears to be due to the fact that the internal representatives identify themselves in most cases with the interests of the enterprise, because as a rule they have held important positions within the enterprise for many years and have amassed great experience and expertise on conditions within the enterprise and within the plants. To counteract the tendency towards too much enterprise or plant egotism on the part of this group, there is the external representation which introduces a wider view of the general economic interest.

These investigations showed that the 'interest of the employees in the continued prosperity of the enterprise was never less than that of the shareholders or owners' (Mitbestimmung . . . , pp. 31–4).

Although the internal representatives usually belonged to trade unions, and their choice and those of the external representatives is normally the result of intense consultation between works councils and trade unions represented in the enterprise, there were frequent conflicts between trade union representatives and internal representatives from the enterprise.

The essential advantage which co-determination in supervisory boards secures to the employees, in so far as their representatives are willing and able to achieve it, is to give them more information about the development of the firm and about the structure of decision-making. The social concerns of the workforce could be more fully taken into consideration and hardships arising for individuals from redundancies and schemes of rationalisation could be alleviated through appropriate social measures.

Worker participation in the sense of influence on decision-making within an enterprise is restricted by the legal limitation of co-determination to personnel and social matters. In many cases, even the available scope for participation is not fully exploited; and, even if it is, the purpose is not always to safeguard the immediate interests of the employees but very often the interests of the representative bodies which for various reasons take on a life very much of their own.

The experience of co-determination on the basis of the Works Constitution Act is similar. The works council, in practice, turns out to be an organ of mediation between the workforce and the employer.

APPENDIX

TABLE 6.1a   Loss of working days per 100 employed persons through strikes and lockouts

	1954	1955	1956	1957	1958	1959	1960	1961	1962	1963
FRG	9.9	3.1	9.0	5.9	4.2	0.3	0.2	0.3	2.2	8.7
France	11.9	25.1	11.4	32.6	9.0	15.3	8.4	20.0	14.2	43.9
Italy	58.6	60.6	42.5	45.2	38.7	83.9	50.3	83.8	186.8	91.1
Belgium	18.0	39.6	36.8	144.9	11.4	38.3	12.9	3.5	10.0	9.0
Gt. Britain	11.5	17.4	9.5	38.3	15.9	24.1	13.6	13.5	25.4	7.7
U.S.A.	45.3	54.5	61.9	30.4	45.1	126.5	34.2	29.1	32.4	27.4

SOURCE   E. Schmidt [1972] p.48.

TABLE 6.1b   The major industrial disputes in FRG, 1950–71

Year		Participants* ('000)	Duration
1950	Strike of building workers in Hesse	10	2 weeks
1951	Strike of agricultural workers in Lower Saxony	12	10 days
	Strike of engineering workers in Hesse	80	4 weeks
1952	Demonstration strike of newspaper printers in FRG		2 days
	Strike in the printing industry in FRG	80	9 days
1953	Strike of shipyard workers in Bremen	14	6 weeks
	Strike of textile workers in Northrhine-Westphalia and Lower Saxony	22	6 weeks
1954	Strike of municipal workers in Hamburg	13	8 days
	Strike of engineering workers in Bavaria	100	3 weeks
1955	Protest strike in the coal and steel industry	800	1 day
1956	Strike of wood workers in Westphalia	15	2 weeks
1956/7	Strike of engineering workers in Schleswig-Holstein	30	16 weeks
1958	Strike of textile workers in Lower Saxony and Hesse	15	9 weeks
	Strike of municipal workers in FRG	200	1 day
1962	Strike of miners in the Saar	40	8 days
	Strike of paper workers (in the Union of Chemical, Paper and Ceramics) in several Lände	8	3 weeks
1963	Strike of engineering workers in Baden-Wüttemberg (including lockout)	350	2 weeks
1967	Strike of floorstone layers in Northrine-Westphalia	6	9 weeks
	Strike of rubber workers in Hesse	10	1 week
1971	Strike of chemical workers in several Lände	50	4 weeks
	Strike of engineering workers in Baden-Wüttemberg (including lockout)	360	3 weeks

* In view of the incomplete statistics from official and trade union sources, the figures for participants must be taken as orders of magnitude rather than as exact figures. For the most part they have been taken from the Reports of the Trade Unions concerned and then compared with the official statistics (*Stat. Bundesamt*, Fachserie A, Reihe 6, III, Streiks). Further sources: H. Grote, *Der Streik–Strategie und Taktik* (Köln, 1952); Th. Pirker, *Die blinde Macht*, 2 Bde. (Munchen, 1960); R. Kalbitz, *Die Arbeitskampfe in der BRD–Aussperrung und Streik 1948–1968*, duplicated research report, Bochum 1972.

SOURCE   J. Bergmann [1975] p. 210.

TABLE 6.1c   Industrial disputes (strikes and lockouts) in six European countries, 1951–70 (annual average, '000)

Country	Participants		Days lost	
	1951–60	*1961–70*	*1951–60*	*1961–70*
Italy	1,980	3,508	5,278	15,247
Gt. Britain	715	1,456	3,416	4,350
		2,021*		2,509*
France	1,950	3,021†	2,916	17,509†
FRG	133	98	949	321
Netherlands	20	15	106	49
Sweden	6	7	149	69

* Excluding May/June 1968, for which there are no official statistics
† Including estimated values for May/June 1968.
SOURCE DGB Strike Statistics in the ILO *Year Book of Labour Statistics.*

TABLE 6.1d   Strikes and lockouts in the FRG 1950–73

Year	Employees involved ('000)	Days lost ('000)
1950	79	380
1951	174	1,593
1952	85	443
1953	51	1,488
1954	116	1,586
1955	597	847
1956	25	264
1957	45	2,386
1958	202	780
1959	22	62
1960	17	38
1961	21	65
1962	79	451
1963	317	1,846
1964	6	17
1965	6	49
1966	196	27
1967	60	389
1968	25	25
1969	90	249
1970	184	93
1971	536	4,484
1972	23	66
1973	185	563

NOTE Figures are rounded up to the nearest thousand. In strike statistics, strikes with less than 10 employees or of less than a day's duration are not included unless more than 100 working days were lost in consequence.

SOURCE *Statistische jahrbücher für die Bundesrepublik Deutschland*, 1952–73.

TABLE 6.1e   Development of unofficial strikes in FRG, 1949–68

Period	Unofficial strikes as % of all strikes	Participants in unofficial strikes as % participants in all strikes	Lost days in unofficial strikes as % of lost days in all strikes
1949–53	42.0	11.6	4.9
1954–58	45.8	6.4	3.7
1959–63	63.9	47.9	7.5
1964–68	83.3	66.0	29.7

SOURCE R. Kalbitz, 'Die Entwicklung von Streiks und Aussperrungen in der BRD, in 0. Jacobi, W. Müller-Jentseh, E. Schmidt (eds), *Gewerkschaften und Klassenkampf, Kritisches Jahrbuch 1973* (Frankfurt am Main, 1973) p. 174.

TABLE 6.2a   Wage share in FRG 1950–72

	Actual wage share	Calculated Wage Share	
		Modified wage share 1	Modified wage share 2
1950	58.6	58.6	58.6
1951	58.7	59.7	57.6
1952	57.4	60.5	55.7
1953	58.7	61.4	56.0
1954	59.4	62.2	55.9
1955	58.8	63.2	54.5
1956	59.5	64.0	54.5
1957	59.7	64.4	54.3
1958	60.5	64.6	54.9
1959	60.2	65.2	54.2
1960	60.6	66.4	53.7
1961	62.2	67.1	54.6
1962	64.0	67.6	55.6
1963	64.4	68.2	55.5
1964	64.3	68.7	55.0
1965	64.7	69.2	55.0
1966	65.7	69.5	55.6
1967	65.9	69.4	56.0
1968	63.9	69.7	54.0
1969	65.4	70.3	54.7
1970	67.0	71.0	55.6
1971	68.8	71.2	56.8
1972	69.2	71.5	

NOTE 1950–59: Federal Area excluding Saar and Berlin (West); 1960–72: Federal Area including Saar and Berlin (West).

SOURCES Sachverständigenrat, *Jahresgutachien 1965*, p.58, Table 30; Sachverständigenrat, *Jahresgutachien 1971*, p.36, Table 9; Deutsche Bundesbank, *Geschäftsbericht fur das Jahr 1972* (Frankfurt, 1973) p. 9.

TABLE 6.2b   Growth of wage share (% change against previous year)

	Actual wage share	Modified wage share 1
1951	+0.2	+1.9
1952	−2.2	+1.3
1953	+2.3	+1.5
1954	+1.2	+1.3
1955	−1.0	+1.6
1956	+1.2	+1.3
1957	+0.3	+0.6
1958	+1.3	+0.3
1959	−0.5	+0.9
1960	+0.7	+1.8
1961	+2.6	+1.1
1962	+2.9	+0.7
1963	+0.6	+0.9
1964	−0.2	+0.7
1965	+0.6	+0.7
1966	+1.5	+0.4
1967	+0.3	−0.1
1968	−3.0	+0.4
1969	+2.3	+0.9
1970	+2.4	+1.0
1971	+2.7	+0.3

SOURCE J. Bergmann [1975] p. 357 (author's calculations).

TABLE 6.2c   Wage agreements in the engineering industry since 1956

Base line	Date of increment	% of rise	Wage rise equivalent to reduction in hours (%)
Bremen Agreement*	1.10.56	1.3	6.7
Bad Soden Agreement			
1	1. 1.58	6	
2	1. 1.59		2.3
Wage Movement 1959	in 1959	4.6	
Bad Homburg Agreement			
1	1. 7.60	8.5	
2	1. 7.61	5.0	
3	1. 1.62		3.5
4	1. 1.64		3.0
Wage Movement 1962	1. 1.62	6.0	
Wage Movement 1963			
1	1. 4.63	5.0	
2	1. 4.64	2.0	
First Erbach Agreement			
1	1.10.64	6.0	
2	1. 7.65	3.0	
Second Erbach Agreement			
1	1. 1.66	6.0	
2	1. 1.67	1.9	3.1
Bad Nauheim Agreement			
1	1. 4.68	4.0	
2	1. 1.69	3.0	
Frankfurt Agreement	1. 9.69	8.0	
Wage Movement 1970	1.10.70	15.3†	
Wage Movement 1971	1. 1.72	7.5	
Wage Movement 1972/3	1. 1.73	8.5	
Wage Movement 1974			
1	1. 1.74	11.0	
2	1.11.74	2.0	

* Agreements are centrally negotiated; wage movements arise, as a rule, on the basis of a regional agreement which serves as a model for other regions and wage districts.

† Average of all wage districts.

TABLE 6.2d   Labour productivity in FRG, 1951–72

Year*	Real gross domestic product per employed person			Real gross domestic product per employee hour			Production per employee-hour
	% Growth (1950=100)			% Growth (1950=100)			
	Annual	Average per cycle		Annual	Average per cycle		
1951	7.7		108	8.2		108	
1952	6.9	6.8	115	6.9	7.0	116	
1953	5.7		122	5.9		123	
1954	4.9		128	5.6		130	
1955	8.0		138	8.2		140	
1956	4.4	4.8	144	3.6	5.6	145	
1957	3.4		149	6.1		154	
1958	3.2		154	4.3		160	
1959	6.4		163	7.3		173	
1960	7.1		175	6.7		184	8.9
1961	4.2	4.8	183	5.5	5.9	193	5.7
1962	3.3		189	5.2		203	7.1
1963	3.0		194	4.6		213	6.2
1964	6.3		207	6.2		226	9.0
1965	4.9	4.3	217	5.3	4.9	238	5.4
1966	3.1		223	3.5		247	4.8
1967	2.9		230	4.6		258	8.1

TABLE 6.2d (continued)

Year*	Real gross domestic product per employed person			Real gross domestic product per employee hour			Production per employee-hour
	% Growth (1950=100)			% Growth (1950=100)			
	Annual	Average per cycle		Annual	Average per cycle		
1968	6.9		246	6.8		275	8.6
1969	6.2		261	7.1		295	7.1
1970	4.4	4.8	272	4.6	5.2	308	3.4
1971	2.7		279	3.6		319	6.6
1972	3.8		290	4.1		332	
Average yearly rate of change							
1951–72	5.0			5.6			1960–71 6.7

* Federal area from 1960 including Saar and Berlin (West)
SOURCE   Statistisches Bundesamt, *Wirtschaft und Statistik sowie Jahreswirtschaftsberichte der Bundesregierung.* *Eigene Berechnungen.*

TABLE 6.2e Real productivity and real wage income in the FRG, 1951–72

| | Real gross domestic product per employed person % Growth | | Wage and salary amounts per employed person | | | |
| | | | Gross | | Net | |
Year	Annual	Average per cycle	Annual	Average per cycle	Annual	Average per cycle
1951	7.7		8.0		6.2	
1952	6.9	6.8	5.7	7.2	5.0	6.5
1953	5.7		7.8		8.3	
1954	4.9		5.0		5.3	
1955	8.0		6.2		6.0	
1956	4.4	4.8	5.4	4.8	4.9	4.6
1957	3.4		3.1		3.7	
1958	3.2		4.4		3.2	
1959	6.4		4.5		4.8	
1960	7.1		7.9		6.5	
1961	4.2	4.8	7.7	5.8	6.8	5.2
1962	3.3		5.8		5.3	
1963	3.0		3.0		2.5	
1964	6.3		6.5		5.9	
1965	4.9	4.3	5.4	4.3	6.3	4.0
1966	3.1		3.6		2.2	
1967	2.9		1.8		1.4	

TABLE 6.2e   (continued)

	Real gross domestic product per employed person		Wage and salary amounts per employed person			
		% Growth	Gross		Net	
	Annual	Average per cycle	Annual	Average per cycle	% Growth Annual	Average per cycle
1968	6.9		4.5		3.2	
1969	6.2		6.2		4.5	
1970	4.4	4.8	10.6	6.2	8.1	4.7
1971	2.7		6.2		4.2	
1972	3.8		3.4		3.4	
Average	5.0		5.6		4.9	

SOURCE Own calculations according to the price and Social Product Statistics of the Bundesamtes: *Wirtschaft und Statistik. Sozialbericht 1972*, Bundestagsdrucksache VI, 3432, p. 157.

TABLE 6.2f Relative disadvantage of employees since 1950 — difference between actual wage share and modified wage share 1 in % actual wage share

	Difference (%)	Difference in % of actual wage share
1951	1.0	1.7
1952	3.1	5.4
1953	2.7	4.6
1954	2.8	4.7
1955	4.4	7.5
1956	4.5	7.6
1957	4.7	7.9
1958	4.1	6.8
1959	5.0	8.3
1960	5.8	9.6
1961	4.9	7.9
1962	3.6	5.6
1963	3.8	5.9
1964	4.4	6.8
1965	4.5	7.0
1966	3.8	5.8
1967	3.5	5.3
1968	5.8	9.1
1969	4.9	7.5
1970	4.0	6.0
1971	2.4	3.5

SOURCE J. Bergmann [1975] p. 358 (author's calculations).

TABLE 6.3 Application of the Laws on Capital Formation*

Year	Number of employees		Those receiving employers' contribution		Amount invested		Average amount invested	
	'000	%†	'000	%†	DM m.	%†	DM	%†
1961	50	.	-	-	15	-	300	.
1962	150	+200	-	-	40	+167	267	-11
1963	250	+67	-	-	70	+75	280	+5
1964	380	+52	-	-	100	+43	271	-3
1965	2,200	+479	-	.	620	+520	280	+3
1966	3,200	+45	750	.	900	+45	280	±0
1967	3,700	+16	800	.	1,000	+11	270	-4
1968	4,500	+22	900	.	1,200	+20	267	-1
1969	5,700	+27	1,000	.	1,600	+33	280	+5
1970	12,100	+112	7,600	+660	3,900	+144	322	+15
1971	15,100	+25	11,200	+47	7,000	+80	465	+44
1972	16,900	+12	12,700	+13	8,700	+24	510	+10
1973	18,200	+8	14,200	+12	9,500	+9	520	+2

* Law for the promotion of capital formation among employees of 12 July 1961 (BGB1, 1, p. 909); Second Law for the promotion of capital formation among employees of 1 July 1965 (BGB1, 1, p. 585) and the Third Law for the promotion of capital formation among employees of 27 June 1970 (BGB1, 1, p. 930) – on the basis of information of Associations of Credit Institutes, of the German Federal Bank and of the Association of Life Insurance Companies, estimated.
† Change from previous year.
SOURCE Bundesminister fur Arbeit und Sozialordnung, Einhommensund Vermogensuerteilung in der Bundesrepublik Deutschland, Ausgabe 1975, p. 157.

TABLE 6.4   Membership of the DGB trade unions and level of unionisation, 1950–73

Year	Dependent Employees* (millions)	Members of DGB unions†	unionisation‡ (%)
1950	15,254	5,450	35.7
1951	15,718	5,980	38.0
1952	16,133	6,004	37.2
1953	16,603	6,051	36.4
1954	17,189	6,103	35.5
1955	17,768	6,105	34.4
1956	18,244	6,125	33.6
1957	18,654	6,244	33.5
1958	18,871	6,332	33.6
1959	18,984	6,274	33.0
1960	20,528	6,379	31.0
1961	20,911	6,382	30.5
1962	21,187	6,430	30.3
1963	21,447	6,431	30.0
1964	21,553	6,485	30.0
1965	21,904	6,574	30.0
1966	21,926	6,537	29.8
1967	21,513	6,408	29.8
1968	21,506	6,376	29.6
1969	21,931	6,482	29.6
1970	22,395	6,713	30.0
1971	22,581	6,869	30.4
1972	22,586	6,986	30.9
1973	22,737	7,168	31.5

* Dependent persons in employment and out of work, 1950–9, excluding Saar and Berlin (West).

† From 1950 Federal area including Berlin (West), including pensioners and unemployed.

‡ The % of unionisation for the years 1950–9 is slightly too high because the figures of dependent employed persons exclude the Saar and Berlin (West).

SOURCE Council of Experts Report for the year 1973, op. cit., p. 206, Table 14; Report of the DGB 1950–1971; Statistical Yearbooks 1952–73; author's calculations.

REFERENCES

Argartz, V. [1953], 'Beitrage zur wirtschaftslichen Entwicklung 1953, Expansive Lohnpolitik', in *W WI–Mitteilungen, Zeitschrift des Wirtschaftswissenschaftlichen Instituts der Gewerkschaften* [Reflections on Economic Development 1953, Dynamic Wages Policy, in WWI–Information, *Journal of the Economic Institute of the Trade Unions*], 6, 12.

Beck-Texte. [1974], *Arbeitsqesetze dtv* [Labour Laws], 16 Edition (Munich).

Bergmann, J., Jacobi, O., and Muller–Jentsch, W. [1975], *Gewerkschaften in der BRD* [Trade Unions in the FRG], EVA, Ffm.

Brenner, Otto, 'Die Zeit nutzen', *Die Quelle, Funktionarzeitschrift des DGB* ['Take the Opportunity', *The Source, Journal for Officials of the DGB*], 6, 10.

Clay, Lucius D. [1950], *Entscheidung in Deutschland* [Decision in Germany], Ffm.

Die Gewerkschaftsbewegung in der Britischen Besatzungszone, Geschaftsbericht des DGB (Brit. Zone) 1947–1949 [1949], [The Trade Union Movement in the British Zone of Occupation, report of the DGB (British Zone) 1947–1949] (Cologne).

Economic Council of the CDU [1973], *Mitbestimmung in Modellen* [Co-determination Models].

Frankfurter Allgemeine Zeitung (FAZ) [1974], no. 19. *The Co-Determination Compromise, Text of the Agreement.*

Geschaftsbericht des DGB 1950/51 [Report of the DGB 1950–51] (Cologne).

Ig Bau-Steine-Erden, Gerwerkschaftstag 1963, Protokoll [Protocol of the Annual Conference of the Construction Union 1963].

Ig Bau-Steine-Erden, Geschaftsbericht 1966–68 [Report 1966–68 of the Union of the Construction Industry].

Leber, Georg [1964], *Vermogensbildung in Arbeitnehmerhand* [Capital Formation for Employees], Documentation 1, Ffm.

Leitsatze der Industriegewerkschaft Metall zur Vermogenspolitik [1972] [Guidelines of the Engineering Union on Wealth Distribution Policies], published in *Metall – Pressedienst* [Engineering Union Press Information], Ffm, no. 7.

Mitbestimmung im Unternehmen, Bericht der Sachverstandigen Kommission zur Auswertung der Bisherigen Erfahrung bei der Mitbestimmung, Deutscher Bundestag – 6. Wahlperiode Drucksache VI, 334. [Co-determination in Enterprises, Report of the Commission of Experts on the Evaluation of Experience in Co-Determination, Sixth Federal Parliament, printed paper VI, 334].

Politik und Programm des DGB [1974], [Policy and Programme of the DGB] (Cologne).

Schmidt, E. [1972], *Ordnungsfaktor oder Gegenmacht. Die politische Rolle der Gewerkschaften* [Agencies of Integration or Countervailing Force. The Political Role of the Trade Unions], Edition Suhrkamp 487, 2nd ed., Ffm.

Wallich, Henry C. [1955], *Die Triebkrafte des deutschen Wiederaufstiegs* [The Dynamics of German Re-construction], Ffm.

Zink, Harold [1957], *The United States in Germany 1944–1955* (Princeton).

7 Trade Union Influence on the Distribution of the Social Product in the Federal German Republic: Wage Policy, Co-determination, Distribution of Wealth and Capital, and Social Security

Fritz Abb

The purpose of this essay is to supplement the discussion about participation and its contradictions. It is concerned with the various forms of action by which the trade unions have sought to influence distribution of the social product in the Federal German Republic.

In principle, there are various forms of action open to the trade unions to influence the distribution of the social product within a capitalist market economy and these actions can be both complementary and alternative. They are: wages policy, co-determination, wealth redistribution, social security. In the Federal German Republic, the trade unions have followed these forms of action with changing priorities. Historically there were three overlapping phases, in each of which one line of action was predominant. The three phases can be roughly characterised as follows:

First phase (economic reconstruction from the currency reform until well into the 1950s): co-determination and social security had priority over wealth redistribution and wages policy.

Second phase (economic consolidation from the mid-1950s until well into the 1960s): wealth redistribution and social security had priority over co-determination and wages policy.

Third phase (end of the 1960s until the mid-1970s). Wages policy and social security had priority over co-determination and wealth redistribution.

Within the fuller exposition of the various phases which follows the author gives his own evaluation of the different policies adopted by trade unions to influence the distribution of the social product within a capitalist market economy.

FIRST PHASE

1. In the first phase of the reconstruction of the German economy after the currency reform and after the restoration of free collective bargaining, the German trade unions pursued a consciously restrained wages policy which according to the predominant view of the public was not directed towards social redistribution but towards integration. A high level of unemployment left no room for an expansive wages policy. This restrained policy on wages, accompanied by a high level of consumer restocking, causing an upward pressure on prices, led to high expectations of profits by private industry with a readiness to invest, mainly on the basis of self-finance. Starting from a low level, the economy reached high growth rates. In competition on international markets the policy of wage restraint by the trade unions created advantages for German exporters which were often felt to amount to 'dumping' abroad. In fact, foreign markets were opened up at this time in which a high German export surplus has been maintained ever since. Trade unions received express recognition from the public for their concern about general economic considerations and their willingness to subordinate their short-term interests. There was, however, growing resistance within the trade union movement to the policy of wage restraint. In particular, Victor Agartz, then director of the Economic Institute of the Trade Unions, demanded from 1953 onwards the pursuit of an expansive wages policy.

2. Rapid capital formation in private industry as a consequence of trade union wage restraint was further enhanced during this first phase through economic, fiscal and competition policies, in order to improve growth rates even more. The result was an uneven distribution of wealth, reinforcing the uneven distribution of the pre-war period which was left unchanged by the currency reform. This uneven distribution was accepted as the consequence of an economic policy based on growth.

3. The trade unions, financed by employees to represent their interests, had difficulty during this first phase to make their restraint acceptable to their members. This is reflected, for example, in the low level of organisation in the German trade union federation, amounting to only about a third of the working population and declining. It was a widely held view that the trade unions were attempting to compensate for their restraint in wages policy and in the distribution of property by the adoption of wide demands for co-determination. It was, in fact, during this phase that the Co-determination Law (1951) and the Works Constitution Law (1952) went into force. It is, however, difficult to show statistically any effect of co-determination on the other forms of social redistribution, wages policy and redistribution of wealth.

4. The first phase of restraint on wages and redistribution of wealth is marked by the attempt of the trade unions to influence policy on social security, in a period when most of the basic social legislation of the Federal German Republic was being passed; the law on wage and salary agreements (1949), protection against dismissal (1951), domestic work (1951), protection of mothers (1952), protection of handicapped persons (1953), provision for war victims (1950), family allowances (1954). During this phase, social benefits and amenities within plants, on which the trade unions had little influence, expanded greatly.

5. The first phase of development can, therefore, correctly be characterised as the phase of co-determination and of social security, instead of wealth redistribution and an expansive wage policy.

SECOND PHASE

1. Although the economy of the Federal Republic reached an advanced degree of development through high growth rates and was approaching full employment, there can be no question of an expansive wage policy by the trade unions during this second phase. The trade unions did, however, demand during this phase important reductions in hours and for the most part, secured them.

2. Compensation for the surrender of an expansive wage policy was sought in a policy of redistribution to counteract the previous development of unequal capital distribution. Table 7.1 shows the inequality of capital formation. Nominal capital formation for each self-employed person between 1950 and 1960, leaving out of account ploughed-back profits, was 5.6 times that for each employee (if ploughed-back profits are taken into account, it was 19.2 times during the period 1950–63). If the claims of employees to social benefits and pensions, which are

TABLE 7.1   Capital formation, 1950–60, in socio-economic categories: nominal capital formation (=capital formation in money and goods) per income recipient (excluding retained profits)

Category	Workers	Salaried employees	Civil servants	Employees	Pensioners	Farmers	Self-employed (excluding farmers)	Totals
DM	1200	3200	4900	(2000)	2200	1800	13,200 (63,200)*	3000
Relationships	0.6	1.6	2.5	(1)	1.1	0.9	6.6 (19.2)*	1.5

* Including retained profits 1950–63.

SOURCE Krelle, W., Schunck, J., Siebke, J., *Überbetriebliche Ertragsbeteiligung der Arbeitnehmer* [Share of Employees in the Social Product] Bd II (Tübingen, 1968) p. 327; Mohr, J. C. B., Ballerstedt, E., Glatzer, W., *Soziologischer Almanach* [Sociological Almanac] (Frankfurt, New York: Herder & Herder, 1975) p. 399.

TABLE 7.2   Capital formation, 1960–3, in socio-economic categories: nominal capital formation (= capital formation in money and goods) per income recipient (excluding retained profits)

Category	Workers	Salaried employees	Civil servants	Employees	Pensioners	Farmers	Self-employed (excluding farmers)	Totals
DM	900	1600	1900	(1300)	700	1600	8800	1700
Relationships	0.7	1.2	1.5	(1)	0.5	1.2	6.8	1.3

SOURCES As Table 7.1.

themselves a result of the social security policy, are taken into account, then this distribution of wealth is approximately as unequal as distribution of income, i.e. the amount owned by a self-employed person is two to three times that owned by an employee. The basis for a more equal distribution of wealth was laid in the laws on capital formation (1961 and 1965), in the social development of the laws on savings premiums and house-building premiums, through the distribution to private owners of Federal industrial property (1959, 1961, 1965) and in a series of other fiscal measures.

During this phase there originated most of the plans to bring about a more even distribution of property: the Gleitze plan (profit-sharing for employees, with compulsory savings), 1957; the Deist plan (profit-sharing by the state, with saving incentives for employees), 1960; the Büttner plan (equal claim of capital and labour to the growth of capital), 1961; the Friedrich plan (interest and tax-free long-term credits to a national fund), 1962; joint Lutheran and Catholic memorandum on property (capital formation through additional wage components agreed in collective bargaining), 1964; and other plans for wage components linked with investment to be either agreed upon by collective bargaining or laid down by law. In academic circles, the Krelle plan for profit-sharing for investment (1968) received considerable attention. The Gleitze and Büttner plans mentioned earlier came from the trade unions. It was especially the trade union in the construction industry, IG Bau-Steine-Erden, which advocated a policy of wealth redistribution on the basis of investment income.

All the measures and plans here mentioned aim to bring about a more equal distribution of property not by redistributing existing wealth, but by ensuring that new capital formation is on a more equal basis, so that in the end the total of property is more equally shared. This has two consequences which call in question the success of plans for wealth redistribution. The more equal sharing of new capital can only take place to a limited extent, otherwise the willingness to invest of those who have to bear the burden, and therefore future growth, is impaired. This in turn means that a perceptible equalisation of total capital formation only comes about after decades. Secondly, the benefit to those favoured by the annual redistribution of capital is so slight that they will be inclined to use these small amounts for consumption, given their existing high propensity to consume (unless one deprives them permanently in some discriminatory fashion of the disposal rights over these amounts), so that a redistribution of wealth does not, in fact, take place. An improvement in the distribution of capital formation through such policies is, in fact, not noticeable (see Table 7.2). Whereas the relationship of capital formation between employees and self-employed persons between 1950 and 1960 was in the proportion of 1 to 6.6 (see Table 7.1), between 1960 and 1963 it rose to 1 to 6.8 (there was some redistribution within the category of employees).

3. These consequences, in the end, produced trade union opposition to giving priority to wealth redistribution. The IG-Metall wanted to see priority given to co-determination instead of redistribution of wealth. Given the obvious difficulties in achieving a more equal distribution of wealth, they took the view that the question of legal ownership was relatively secondary and should not remain at the centre of discussion. It was more important to deal with the management of property through co-determination. In fact, there was little further development in the field of co-determination in this second phase.

4. In contrast, social legislation advanced greatly during this second phase under the influence of the trade unions – reform of pensions (dynamic pensions, 1957); improvements in the sickness insurance of workers (1957); far-reaching changes of unemployment insurance (1956); reform of accident insurance (1963); and the law for the protection of young persons (1957). A number of laws which had come into force in the first phase were improved: family allowances (1964); provision for war victims (1960, 1964, 1966); and provision for handicapped persons (1961).

5. The second phase can, therefore, be rightly called the phase of wealth redistribution and social security instead of co-determination and expansive wage policy.

THIRD PHASE

1. The third phase after the recession of 1966 until the recession of the middle 1970s is marked collective bargaining for an expansive wages policy by the trade unions, following a series of wildcat strikes caused by the fact that wages lagged behind profits when the boom started again. The union leaders had to be more active on the wages front if they were not to lose control of their members. Statistics on strikes show the force of a more expansive wage policy at the beginning of the third phase. '1971 was the year which recorded the highest loss of working days through strikes. . . . the size of industrial disputes was also at its peak in 1971' [Press and Information Office of the Federal Republic, *Data for 1973* (Bonn, 1974) p. 114]. Statistics on incomes distribution also showed the growing importance of expansive wages policy in the third phase. Since the early 1960s there has been a relatively strong rise in the average yearly percentage change in gross income from employment per average employed person (see Table 7.3) compared with the percentage of national income going to wages (not structurally adjusted, see Table

TABLE 7.3   Average annual change in % of Gross Income from dependent employment per average employed person

1950/55	1955/60	1960/65	1965/70	1970/72
+8.6	+7.3	+8.3	+8.4	+11.3

SOURCE Press and Information Office of the Federal Republic (ed.), *Societal Data, 1973* (Bonn, 1974) p. 121.

7.4). The growth of unionisation in the third phase shows that the greater power of an expansive wages policy can be seen as a consequence of the success of trade union activity.

TABLE 7.4   Wage share (gross income from dependent employment as % of national income)

1950	1955	1960	1965	1966	1967	1968	1969	1970	1971	1972	1973	1974
58.6	58.8	60.7	66.6	65.7	66.1	64	65.5	67.5	68.3	68.6	69.5	71.6

SOURCE 7.4   Reports of the German Federal Bank.

2. At the same time, the system of social security was further developed in this third phase at the request of the trade unions. This was mainly done by improvements in existing social legislation: the law on wage agreements (1969); protection against dismissal (1969); protection for mothers (1968); promotion of employment (1969); sickness insurance (1970); and flexible age limits in pensions insurance (1972).

3. The third phase appears to be a phase of wealth redistribution and co-determination as well, because these objectives are at the centre of intensive debate on legislative proposals not yet completed. In addition, there was in this third phase, as a contribution towards the more equal wealth distribution, a new legislative proposal for a law on capital formation (1970); and co-determination at the level of the plant was extended through a new version of the law on the constitution of enterprises (1972). The legislative proposal on capital formation is based on the plans put forward in the second phase and therefore suffers from the disadvantages discussed earlier. A major redistribution of wealth is therefore not to be expected even if this law should be completed at some stage in the future.

4. As for the legislative proposal on co-determination at the level of the enterprise, two problems are at the centre of the debate:

(i) Does the proposal guarantee parity or does it leave to the owners of capital the decisive influence in cases of doubt?
(ii) If parity is in fact guaranteed, what will be the consequences?

If the owners retain the decisive influence in cases of doubt, it is not easy to see in what respect things will have changed from the present state of affairs. The trade unions would then have to consider whether it is worth their while to work for more co-determination of this kind or whether it would be better to concentrate their activity in their proper field of wages policy. This is the opinion of many trade unionists. If parity is, in fact, guaranteed, then the range of action open to the leading management bodies of enterprises is affected. As long as only part of the economy is subject to co-determination with parity, it seems likely that co-determination will not essentially change the system of a capitalist market economy, because of the degree of interdependence which exists, but that the objective of the capitalist market system will dominate even those areas subject to co-determination. Gradual improvements in the social situation of employees may be the consequence; but the trade unions must, for their future policy, ascertain whether the improvements which they can win in this manner will not be outweighed by the loss of freedom of action which will occur as a result of being integrated with the employers' side. A system which integrates the trade unions partly with the employers obscures the conflict of capital and labour as strictly separate parties in the market and this can lead to substantial social disadvantage. The experience of co-determination with parity in the mining industry (Report of the Commission on Co-determination) has shown that so far no substantial change in entrepreneurial initiative can be noted.

5. In fact, no new ideas have occurred in respect of wealth redistribution or co-determination in the third phase because the legislative proposals have so far not been completed. The third phase of the development can, therefore, be suitably characterised as the phase of expansive wages policy and social security instead of co-determination and wealth redistribution.

It can be stated as a final conclusion that within the capitalist market economy of the Federal German Republic wages policy has been a successful field of trade union activity for the purpose of social redistribution. In addition the policy for social security plays, in any case, an important role in social redistribution. Wealth redistribution and co-determination have, so far, only proved supplementary solutions to obtain some satisfaction during phases of wage restraint.

8 Participation and the Nature of the Firm

J. Aldrich

INTRODUCTION

This paper contains observations on workers' participation from the viewpoint of some economic theories of the nature of the firm and, in particular, of the nature of the employment relationship. Economic theorising on the firm has concentrated on the market behaviour of firms, i.e., on the *content* of a certain class of decisions rather than on how, or by whom, decisions are made; even the theory of the co-operative firm, developed by Ward, Vanek and others, is a theory of the market behaviour of such enterprises. The problem of the *internal* viability of a co-operative (or, more generally, a participatory) enterprise does not seem to have attracted very much attention from economists; but when it is recalled that the theory of the firm (co-operative as well as profit-maximising) presupposes that the firm is efficiently organised, the importance of the internal viability of the firm is obvious whilst the claims made on behalf of participation have tended to emphasise changes that follow internal reorganisation; however, organisational factors have been neglected in modern economics (compared with Marshall, say, one of whose 'four agents of production' was organisation!) in favour of market analysis. Recently however organisational factors have come to be emphasised in the treatment of 'managerial slack' and 'X-efficiency', and of course in the theories of the employment relationship to be considered later.

Section 1

It is best to start with some definitions, as 'participation' is often used in a very vague sense: we follow Pateman [1970] in distinguishing degrees of participation and levels of participation:

(*a*) 'Partial participation is a process in which two or more parties influence each other in the making of decisions but the final power to decide rests with one party only.'

(b) 'Full participation is a process where each individual member of a decision-making body has equal power to determine the outcome of decisions.'

(c) 'Lower level participation refers to those management decisions relating to the control of day-to-day shop floor activity.'

(d) 'Higher level participation refers to decisions that relate to the running of the whole enterprise, decisions on investment, marketing and so forth.'

These definitions are not phrased in terms of participatory machinery – for example, trade unions, works councils, worker membership of managerial boards and so on – and this is a disadvantage as it makes the discussion remote from programmes of institutional reform; but it is at this level of abstraction that the economic theories that will be considered here have some bearing.

The theories of the employment relationship to be considered here fit rather neatly into a Paretian welfare economics framework, but many of the arguments for or against participation do not fit so easily into this framework; in fact, the criteria implicit in many arguments for participation are incommensurable with those used by economists. Of course, the problem of participation has been examined from the viewpoints of several disciplines but the contrast that I would like to bring out is between the criteria used by Mill [1970] in the chapters on Socialism and by Cole [1972] and those used in formal welfare economics – whether of the utilitarian or Paretian variety. There is a good account of the theories of Mill and Cole in Pateman's book. Most of these points have been made before in discussions of utilitarianism, liberalism and democracy but they seem worth translating into the terms of the present problem. The contrast between these two points of view is quite stark, and permits clear distinctions; but on the other hand, it could be argued that welfare criteria were devised for use on a narrow range of problems (the evaluation of exchange, in the case of Pareto optimality) and that they represent no more than a caricature of economists' deeper thinking on economic philosophy – this point is reinforced by the fact that both men contrasted with the 'welfare economists' were themselves economists! However, the point of view of welfare economics has had an influence far beyond formal welfare economics and it is illuminating to show just how big the differences are. It should not be thought that there were no important differences between the views of Cole and Mill. On the contrary, the kind of participatory economy envisaged by each was quite different: Mill envisaged a system of competitive co-operatives, similar to that studied recently by Vanek, whilst Cole envisaged political – rather than market – links between firms, and the weight of their arguments for participation were placed at different points. It is possible to indicate four main points of contrast between the 'participation view' and the 'welfare economics view':

(i) the ethical theory of the welfare economists is 'consequentialist' whilst that of the participation theorists is not primarily so;

(ii) when consequences *are* discussed, the participation theorists emphasise consequences that cannot easily be evaluated in a welfare economics framework;

(iii) those consequences that *can* be discussed in both frameworks are given different weights;

(iv) there are differences about what the consequences of participation *would be*.

This four-point framework will be quite difficult to maintain as the two views being contrasted form coherent ideologies, with their various parts providing mutual support, so some damage is done to the views by this rather arbitrary division.

(*a*) 'Very roughly speaking, consequentialism is the doctrine that the moral value of any action always lies in its consequences, and that it is by reference to their consequences that actions, and indeed such things as institutions, laws and practices, are to be so justified if they can be justified at all!' (Williams [1973] p. 79). Williams spends about fifteen pages tightening up this definition, as the notions of 'consequence' and 'action' are extremely slack. Welfare economics is a form of consequentialism that takes into account only the effects of actions on individuals' 'utility' levels; and *given* the content of a decision, the identity of the decision-makers is irrelevant unless there are costs and benefits attached to the distribution of decision-making, e.g. if person A likes taking decisions, or if B does not like C taking decisions, and so on. Although the theorists of participation expect different decisions to be made with participation, they emphasise that it is intrinsically good for individuals to have a say in what they are going to do. This attitude is brought out in the following quotations from Cole [1972] p. 44: 'The crying need of our days is the need for freedom. Machinery and Capitalism between them have made the worker a mere serf, with no interest in the product of his own labour beyond the adequate wage which he secures by it'; and on p. 51, 'we can only destroy the tyranny of machinery – which is not the same as destroying machinery itself – by giving into the hands of the workers the control of their life and work, by freeing them to choose whether they will make well or ill, whether they will do the work of slaves or of free men.' (The emphasis on freedom is shared with modern liberals such as Hayek; Rowley and Peacock [1975] have produced a liberal critique of Paretian welfare economics.)

(*b*) One of the consequences of increased participation expected by the participation theorists is that workers would have a greater 'sense of personal worth and dignity' and would be less selfish and more public-spirited. I think that these effects should be construed as changes of tastes, in which case the Paretian principle is in difficulty, although the same is not true of Pigovian or utilitarian welfare economics. Caution is necessary here as it is a basic canon of welfare economics that the content of a person's tastes is an empirical matter, and it could be argued that the change in behaviour expected from participation is merely a rational adaptation to changed circumstances. It seems that the participation theorists would regard the change as a change in tastes, in the sense that an individual faced with the same opportunities would make a different choice as well as feeling different. As Pateman remarks, the participation theorists are much more willing to discuss the effects of institutions on personality than are the welfare economists, and the latter's reluctance can be attributed to the kinds of issues dealt with in formal welfare economics where taste changes do not seem important, to the view that the engineering of tastes is potentially totalitarian or to a scepticism about the likelihood of taste changes. But economists have not always been reluctant to discuss the effects of actions on personality: 'The understandings of the greater part of men are necessarily formed by their ordinary employments. The man whose whole life is spent in performing a few simple operations of which the effects are, perhaps, always the same or very nearly the same, has no occasion to exert his understanding, or to exercise his invention in finding out expedients for removing difficulties that never occur. . . . The torpor of his mind renders him, not only incapable of relishing or bearing a part in any rational conversation but of conceiving any generous, noble or tender sentiment, and consequently of forming any just judgement concerning many even of the ordinary duties of private life.' Smith [1904] vol. 2, p. 302.

(*c*) Whether or not a new-found sense of personal worth connotes a change of taste, it can be asked whether the person involved is on a higher utility level. Mill [1910] claims that it is 'better to be Socrates dissatisfied than a fool satisfied' (p. 9), but his argument that 'better' here means that one would be happier seems distinctly weak; and similarly a claim that somebody has a greater sense of personal worth and dignity neither implies nor is implied by the claim that he is happier. Many of these contrasts involve Mill, as the phrase 'sense of personal worth and dignity' come from his *Principles* (p. 134) and it seems impossible to reconcile his scattered arguments. Apropos of the point made under (*a*), Mill combined the two doctrines of utilitarianism and liberalism, which, though distinct, were in alliance during his lifetime. One of the drawbacks of the success of welfare economics has been a tendency to regard early claims about the reasonable working of the market as clumsy attempts at later 'theorems' when they were often different arguments based on different value premises. Much of the distinctive ethical concerns of earlier writers has been simply forgotten.

One of the consequences of increased participation is increased participation! There is no necessity for a welfare economist to say *a priori* whether this is good or bad, as it all depends on the tastes of the individuals. However, as welfare economists attach no separate importance to *who* takes decisions, their subjects can be expected to be equally rational and so *they* would regard participation as costly—Buchanan and Tullock's 'cost of decision-making'—a necessary cost perhaps if the alternative is a denial of the subjects' interest. Although participation can have unpleasant aspects, for the participation theorists it is both a duty of the responsible worker and a source of a sense of community not otherwise obtainable.

(*d*) By now it should be clear that underlying these two outlooks are very different views of human nature both in terms of what human beings are ultimately for and how they will behave. As a matter of logic, the criteria of welfare economics do not comprise a theory of human behaviour – what people's tastes *are* is a matter of fact and they just have to be fed into the computer to derive an optimal policy. However, as a matter of historical fact, welfare economists have held a particular view of human nature and it is not clear that the welfare economics criteria would make much sense with a very different view of human nature; could one, for example be a utilitarian if all human beings were extreme masochists, would that be a possible ethical position? On top ′of this there are obvious differences in the predictions implicit in the work of welfare economists and in those of participation theorists, summed up by saying that participation theorists think that participatory institutions are viable but welfare economists are sceptical. Two of the participation theorists discussed by Pateman, Mill and Cole, are very clearly libertarians and for the viability of their institutions something like Pareto optimality would be required, as otherwise the participants would make other arrangements. Mill's famous chapter 'On the Probable Futurity of the Labouring Classes' envisages the withering away of the capitalist firm and its replacement by the workers' co-operative as a result of the superior efficiency of the latter; the failure of this prediction is, of course, one reason for the neglect of the economics of co-operatives until the contemporary Yugoslav developments.

I hope that this somewhat schematic treatment has clarified more than it has distorted; it may be argued that the cases contrasted here are figments of my imagination and for the 'welfare economists' ' case this is basically true. There, we have a set of criteria applied by economists to a narrow range of problems, so perhaps I am unreasonably projecting these criteria on to a much wider range of problems. There seem to be the following alternatives: not to discuss these wider questions; to discuss these wider questions within the same framework as the narrower questions; or to discuss these questions within a different framework – my comparison has been between these last two alternatives but the first alternative has been that most often chosen. Once when it was felt that Paretian welfare economics was scientific in line with positivistic methodology it was natural to dismiss other ways of judging social arrangements as nonsensical. By now, these claims have been exploded and the Paretian principle stands as one principle amongst many others; if certain discussions are beyond its scope that must be a serious weakness.

SECTION 2

The theories that we now turn to attempt to explain the existence of the employment relationship – a relationship in which the worker, in exchange for some remuneration, agrees to follow, within certain limits, the instructions of his employer. The relationship, so conceived, appears to admit no degree of participation whatsoever; and so, perhaps, these theories will indicate some of the problems of replacing this relationship by one allowing greater participation. The problem to which these theories are addressed is posed by Coase [1953] in the following terms: 'In view of the fact that while economists treat the price mechanism as a co-ordinating instrument, they also admit the co-ordinating function of the "entrepreneur" it is surely important to enquire why co-ordination is the work of the price mechanism is one case and of the entrepreneur in another' (p. 334).

It is interesting that only two forms of co-ordination are considered – the market system or the command system – and the form of co-ordination urged by Cole and Mill, co-operation, is not considered. The reason is simple: with the possible exception of the family, these have been the dominant forms of economic organisation in the West since the decline of feudalism. However, in the interestices of the market and command systems lie business partnership, shareholding and gang-working, all of which involve non-market, non-command relationships as well as non-economic institutions that are organised on different principles. Sometimes even the command element is denied: 'The single consumer can assign his grocer to the task of obtaining whatever the customer can induce the grocer to provide at a price acceptable to both parties. That is precisely all that an employer can do to an employee. To speak of managing, directing or assigning workers to various tasks is a deceptive way of noting that the employer is involved in renegotiation of contracts on terms that must be acceptable to both parties' (Alchian and Demsetz [1972] p. 777). Although we see later that there *is* a constant renegotiation of contracts, it is quite misleading to imply that employers do *not* 'manage, direct . . . ' .

Coase's answer to his question is that the choice between market co-ordination and entrepreneurial co-ordination depends on which is more efficient, and two sorts of considerations have often been advanced: effects on incentives and economies of scale – 'Writers on social science from the time of Plato downwards have delighted to dwell on the increased efficiency which labour derives from organization' (Marshall [1920] p. 200). Incentives will be discussed later; and as technological economies of scale are familiar, it is worth discussing informational economies of scale; Stiglitz has distinguished two kinds in the context of supervision but his discussion is much more generally relevant: '. . . there are two non-convexities associated with information. The first is that the value of a given amount of information increases with how frequently it can be used; that is, even if the initial cost of acquisition of information of the employee and the supervisor were the same, in a hierarchical structure the supervisor uses the information more fre-quently. . . . Secondly, it can be shown that in general, it does not pay to acquire just a little bit of information: i.e., the costs always exceed the benefits. Thus it does not pay to monitor just a little, it either pays not to monitor at all or to monitor at a finite level', page 575. It may be remarked that Coase [1953], Simon [1957] and Williamson *et al.* [1975] have all pointed to the difficulty of writing sufficiently elaborate contracts as the reason for exploitation of these economies, through organisation rather than through the market. The implication of the existence of these economies of scale for participation is that full participation beyond the lower level is inefficient as it would mean forgoing these advantages. It is natural, therefore, to try to combine the advantages of organisation with participation through representative institutions and this is a feature of all participation schemes where the business of the firm has any complexity. The advantages conferred on the management (or 'technostructure') *vis-à-vis* the owners of the firm by a monopoly of information also apply to the position of the manage-ment *vis-à-vis* the workers, although the latter have the advantage that being within the organisation they have collectively a great deal of information but the assembly of this information may be prohibitively expensive. Stiglitz's second point could also support a policy of 'rational apathy' on the part of the worker (or small shareholder, come to that): that the returns to the individual of becoming better informed are not worth the trouble and unless the returns become large – as they would, for example in the case of the imminent collapse of the firm – he will not take the trouble (cf. Downs on political participation). It is also likely that the worker will be more interested in his day-to-day environment than the running of other departments unless, and until, the latter affects him.

A factor related to information is the possession of different skills, a perspective on which is provided by Marglin [1975].

The ability to organize production – an ability that reflects a mixture of wit, knowledge, leadership, greed and other qualities inherited and acquired – is a public good *par excellence*. The entrepreneur who shares this ability with others – for example his employees – does not thereby diminish his own stock of this ability. He 'merely' diminishes the reward that he can reap from this ability.

However, the sharing of this ability proceeds by giving orders, advice, or by training other entrepreneurs – he cannot divide his ability between his workforce so that the work of co-ordination does itself. The classic works of Marshall [1920] and Knight [1965] emphasise that the entrepreneur needs not only certain abilities but also a willingness to use those abilities and take responsibility if things go wrong; but this matter will be discussed further below.

The model of supervision devised by Alchian and Demsetz [1972] is a useful bridge from the information theories to the incentive theories. The situation envisaged is one in which lack of separability of the production process makes individual contributions to output difficult to identify, thus preventing workers from selling their output. In the absence of supervision, there is an incentive for each member of the gang to shirk because, for him, the impact of a reduction of effort is greater than the loss in the gang's output and consequent loss of earnings. But each worker is in this position (a form of Prisoner's Dilemma) and would be prepared to have a supervisor enforce a higher level of effort on all concerned; assuming, that is, that it is feasible to observe individual efforts. Of course, it may be feasible for the workers to supervise each other; indeed it was at this level of organisation that Marshall [1920] expected co-operatives to excel: 'They render unnecessary some of the minor work of superintendence that is required in other establishments; for their own pecuniary interests and the pride they take in the success of their own business makes each of them adverse to any shirking of work either by himself or by his fellow work-men' (p. 255). Even within capitalist firms, group payment schemes are common, and some of the possible effects on discipline are brought out in the following account of the London docks in the late 1960s: 'It was not unknown to rely on the unions to deal with minor breaches of working rule, through their internal procedure. For instance under piecework and the gang system, one man's delinquency was often as harmful to his mates as the employer and it was simpler for both sides to "branch" the offender than go to the board. Thus the TGWU could fine a man £5 (now £10) for disobeying a ganger's order, coming back drunk after lunch or "pitching off a job without a by-your-leave or thank you" ' (Wilson [1972]). Some jobs are organised to permit a very high degree of low-level partici-pation, these arrangements being common in mining, forestry and elsewhere; although most factory jobs are designed, there may be limited scope for allowing job autonomy without large output losses. Cole [1973] argued that 'collective contracts' between an owner of a plant and the workers who take responsibility for producing an agreed level of output using that plant are a useful move towards workers' control of industry; in parts of the nineteenth century, industry arrangements of this kind were common except that skilled workers would recruit and supervise their own unskilled helpers, which did not provide very much participation for the latter—see Bendix [1956] and Stone [1973]. This work suggests a further reason for neglecting co-operation as an alternative to market and command, in the view that it works best when small numbers of people are involved whereas markets and hierarchies can handle almost any amount of business—although, in the case of hierarchies, subject to some control loss at the top. Command, however, is mediated through hierarchies and in the sort of guild socialism scheme envisaged by Cole co-operation would also be arranged through a sequence of higher-level institutions. One possible explanation is that co-operation is based on trust and this is difficult to achieve outside small face-to-face situations and is unstable in that in such small-number situations the cost of a breakdown in trust is quite severe, whereas in markets (with large numbers) trust is not important. Command systems have something of the impersonality of markets in that the emotional commitment is limited on both sides.

The other main consideration for participation, derived from theories of the nature of the firm, is the pattern of incentives — especially as this affects risk-taking. Both Marshall [1920] and Knight [1965] emphasise the importance of clearly delineated responsibility for decisions; indeed, for Marshall this is one of the potential weaknesses of joint-stock companies. More recently, this problem has been dealt with by Arrow, Stiglitz and others under the name moral hazard: 'With conventional risk-sharing, there is likely to be a reduction in incentives (known as moral hazard in the insurance literature)' (Stiglitz [1975]). By contrast with Alchian and Demsetz [1972], Marshall and Knight are concerned with initiatives rather than routine supervision: 'Wherever we find an apparent separation between control and uncertainty bearing, examination will show that we are confusing essentially routine activities with real control' (Knight [1965] p. 298). In an organisation with specialisation of function a major source of uncertainty is how well a subordinate will do his job, and Marshall in particular has emphasised the problems that were faced by a co-operative in choosing managerial personnel. The moral hazard argument is that by sharing the risks attending a decision the decision-makers will be less careful in exercising their judgement; if Marglin's entrepreneur were to advise the employees about the best course of action would he be as careful about the quality of his advice as if his reward or penalty were closely linked to its outcome; and conversely, if his reward (or penalty) were so linked would he take on the responsibility without control?

SECTION 3

In this last section, it is intended to discuss some of the limitations of these analyses of the employment relation. As remarked above, the notion of the employment relation studied admits very limited participation – essentially either side can withdraw from the deal and the impression conveyed by the passage quoted from Alchian and Demsetz is that this is the main option. In fact, this is not the only option; to use Hirschman's vivid terminology, a 'voice' option exists as well as an 'exit' option and, in practice, the former is very important in employment relations. The more expensive it is, on either side, to form new contracts elsewhere, the less attractive is the exit option; all non-casual relationships will evolve means for dealing with grievances and other matters (for changing jobs and finding and training new employees are not costless operations) – both parties have much less room to manœuvre than Alchian and Demsetz imply. As a last resort, exit is available on either side, but participatory institutions will develop within the firm; even strike or lockout action is not exit, or the threat of exit, as the implication is that the workers will *return* on better terms. The 'renegotiation of contracts' mentioned by Alchian and Demsetz cannot proceed without the articulation of terms. Although any form of participation could be regarded as a loss of managerial prerogative and therefore, since this is a form of power, as a loss of an asset that could be used for future bargaining with workers, it may be in the employer's interest to allow this; cf. the following account of the replacement of skilled by unskilled workers ('dilution') during the First World War:

> There can be no doubt that, on the whole, the existence of comparatively strong workshop organization in most branches of the munitions industries enabled the dilution to proceed more smoothly than it would otherwise have done . . . it is also true that, if the workers had merely allowed the employers to introduce as much dilution as they might choose how and when they like, the process of dilution would have been far smoother than it actually was. This, however was never really a possibility. The alternative to the regulation of the processes of dilution by the shop stewards would have been an indiscriminate mass opposition in the workshops to dilution in all its forms' (Cole [1973] p. 55).

Participation is present in all on-going relationships. It has been said that collective bargaining is a form of industrial rule-making and 'that even when the subjects covered by collective agreements penetrate deeply into the managerial function, the responsibility accepted by trade unions in signing them does not go beyond upholding the observance of the rules that they have helped to make. Management as a result may have to conduct itself within the limits set by these rules, but otherwise its responsibility for running the business remains undivided' (Flanders [1969] p. 35). Clearly, this is a form of participation in the sense that the workers, through their representatives, have had a hand in deciding the rules that govern their working lives. However, collective bargaining is limited in scope in that some management functions are regarded as managerial prerogatives, and however tightly specified the rules there will be need for their day-to-day interpretation and modification: this is just the obverse of Simon's argument for the employment relation rather than a sale of services–the uncertainty about what is required favours discretion rather than an elaborate contract.

The fact referred to above, that the employment relation is more permanent than these theories have supposed, has important consequences. For various reasons (including the need for incentives), firms have developed internal labour markets and generally a situation has developed in which for many workers their prospects, as well as current position, are better with their present employer than with some other employer. (Williamson *et al.* [1975] have discussed this development in general, and Stone [1973] has treated the evolution of job structures within the U.S. steel industry from the nineteenth century.) However, an individual's prospects depend on factors beyond his control, both inside and outside the firm, and he will want to bring some of these factors under his control. The model of the firm used by Knight, in which risk-bearing is concentrated in the ownership and high managerial positions of the firm, does not fit a situation in which workers have virtual property rights in jobs, for they may face considerable 'capital uncertainty' and they are in a much weaker position to diversify their asset-holding than are shareholders; many workers do not have savings and normally cannot hold several jobs. When an identical job is available elsewhere, the worker has no interest in how well the firm is run but when he has an *interest* in the firm he wants that interest protected. It could be that this interest is best served by letting the management get on with the job subject to certain constraints, in the form of collectively agreed rules. It can be argued that the present division of control within the firm reflects the size of the workers' interest within the firm, that typically the manager will have a larger interest in the firm than the manual worker and that this is reflected in his greater control. No doubt there is force in this argument, especially when it is recalled that the more control an individual has, the more able he is to develop an interest in the firm; however, it puts the division of risk-sharing between shareholders and employees of all kinds in rather a different light.

REFERENCES

Alchian, A., and Demsetz, H. [1972], 'Production, Information Costs and Economic Organization', *American Economic Review*, vol. 62 no. 1, pp. 777–95.

Bendix, R., [1956], *Work and Authority in Industry* (New York: John Wiley).

Buchanan, J. M., and Tullock, G. [1962], *The Calculus of Consent* (Ann Arbor: University of Michigan).

Coase, R. H. [1953], 'The Nature of the Firm' reprinted in *AEA Readings in Price Theory* (Allen & Unwin).

Cole, G. D. H. [1972], *Self-Government in Industry* (Hutchinson).

Cole, G. D. H. [1973], *Workshop Organization* (Hutchinson).

Flanders, A. [1969], 'Collective Bargaining: a theoretical analysis', reprinted in A. Flanders (ed.), *Collective Bargaining. Selected Readings*, (Penguin).

Galbraith, J. K. [1975], *Economics and the Public Purpose* (Penguin).

Hirschman, A. O. [1970], *Exit, Voice and Loyalty* (Harvard University Press).

Knight, F. H. [1965], *Risk, Uncertainty and Profit* (New York: Harper & Row).

Marglin, S. A. [1975], 'What do Bosses do? Postscript', (Harvard Institute of Economic Research, discussion paper).

Marshall, A. [1920], *Principles of Economics* (Macmillan).

Mill, J. S. [1910], *Utilitarianism, Liberty and Representative Government* (Everyman edition).

Mill, J. S. [1970], *Principles of Political Economy* (Penguin).

Pateman, C. [1970], *Participation and Democratic Theory* (Cambridge University Press).

Rowley, C. K., and Peacock, A. T. [1975], *Welfare Economics* (London: Martin Robertson).

Simon, H. A. [1957], 'A Formal Theory of the Employment Relation', reprinted in H. A. Simon, *Models of Man* (New York: John Wiley).

Smith, A. [1904], *The Wealth of Nations*, vol. II (Methuen).

Stiglitz, J. E. [1975], 'Incentives, Risk and Information: notes towards a theory of hierarchy', *Bell Journal of Economics* (autumn 1975) pp. 552–79.

Stone, K. [1973], 'The Origins of Job Structures within the Steel Industry', *Review of Radical Political Economics*, VI, pp. 113–73.

Vanek, J. [1970], *The General Theory of the Labour-Managed Economy* (Ithaca: Cornell University Press).

Ward, B. [1958], 'The Firm in Illyria', *American Economic Review* (Chapter 1 above).

Williams, B. [1973], 'A critique of utilitarianism', *Utilitarianism, for J. J. C. Smart and Bernard Williams and against Cambridge* (Cambridge University Press).

Williamson, O. E., Wachter, M. L., and Harris, J. E. [1975], 'Understanding the employment relation: the analysis of idiosyncratic exchange', *Bell Journal of Economics* (spring) pp. 250–80.

Wilson, D. F. [1972], *Dockers* (Fontana).

9 Participation and Risk[1]

Alan Ingham

1 INTRODUCTION

If an individual participates in the making of some decision, one would expect some cost to be borne because of this. The individual wants to participate so as to attain a position preferred to that in which he does not participate. The position he attains with participation in work decisions may be preferred because the amount of effort consequently devoted, and the level of goods and services he attains, is preferred, or he may like making decisions *per se*. The case where the decision problem is a certain one, that is where one makes a decision and the consequences are known with certainty, is analysed elsewhere in this book. We are here concerned with the case of uncertain consequences of decisions and the implicit consequences for both parties in a bilateral bargaining situation.

In Section 2 we look at three diverse examples of markets in which decisions under uncertainty and various types of legal contracts are entered into. Section 3 outlines the methodology that is applied to the analysis of decision-making under uncertainty, and Section 4 discusses how these ideas can be applied to risk-sharing in one particular market, that of agriculture. Finally we look at some historical evidence on the development of contracts involving participation and risk-sharing. Throughout we have one basic theme: in various economic markets which are in equilibrium, the more an individual participates in decision-making, the more risk he bears. So that how much participation a utility-maximising individual will have, in a market in equilibrium, will depend on his attitude to risk, and individuals who dislike risk intensely may desire to have no participation at all. This perhaps explains the diverse attitude to participation across countries.

2 SOME EXAMPLES OF PARTICIPATION AND RISK

We shall consider participation in decision-making in three different areas, the housing market, the industrial firm, and agriculture. Despite the differences in these situations there is a basic common property that the cost of making decisions is the bearing of risk, or uncertainty, involved with the decisions made. A simple dichotomy for employment in industry is that one can work either for oneself or for an employer. A different amount of risk, arising from different sources, is found in either case. Industrial workers in Western Europe usually find employment with a known wage and conditions of work, but with perhaps uncertain prospects and security of employment. The self-employed on the other hand must worry about sales performance and financial management. He may have greater security than the employee, and is able to choose his conditions of work, but his return may be uncertain. The self-employed thus has a much greater degree of control than the employee. However, it would not necessarily be irrational to work as an employee rather than self-employed, as the utility gained from the knowledge of having a certain wage may well outweigh the disutility of not being able to control one's conditions of work.

One rarely finds secure employment in which hours worked, the length of holiday or job organisation are left to the individual. One notable exception is that of the managers of an enterprise, who are often in full control but not fully responsible for the decisions they take. For example, they are not fully responsible in cases of bankruptcy, the costs of which fall upon the others and creditors. This lack of responsibility is due to the joint stock acts which led to the formation of the modern form of enterprise (see Shannon [1931]). Previous to the joint stock acts the division in an industrial enterprise between managers and workers was between those who made the decisions and took the risks and those who complied with the decisions made but took *relatively* little risk.[2]

The British housing market is a very different topic, yet it yields much the same structure – after all, one could regard the provision of housing services as an industry. Within Britain the population can be broadly divided into two large groups by the type of housing they have (I will exclude those people who own their own houses). One group is people who are buying their own houses and the other consists of those renting houses, either publicly or privately owned. What factors would cause one individual to be buying a house and another to rent? An individual who rents a house, typically, will not have any responsibility for repairs or for the condition of the house, and also has no legal transaction costs associated with moving in or out; however, he may well have to pay a rent determined by market conditions and may have a degree of lack of security of tenure in that he lives in property ultimately belonging to somebody else.

These last two points have limited applicability in Britain today due to legal controls on rent and security of tenure. The individual also has little control over repairs, etc. In contrast, the person buying his own house takes almost exactly, the opposite position to this. The costs of his housing are the repayments on his mortgage, and these can change only through changes in the interest rate.[3] One has security of tenure, and alterations, repairs and other structural alterations are at one's own discretion; although the cost of such maintenance is uncertain, as is the time at which it becomes necessary. There are legal costs involved with purchase and sale and the price at which one could sell in the future is also uncertain. This description is necessarily simplistic but the basic difference between the situation in terms of risk and the amount of control is clear. In the rental case the individual has little participation and the landlord bears risks associated with property, whereas in the purchase case the individual has almost complete control over his house but the building society providing the funds bears little or no risk. Thus the person renting is in a position similar to the employee and the person buying is similar to the self-employed.

The final type of market we wish to consider is that of agricultural employment. Contracts found here will be especially important as it seems to be unusual for tailor-made legal contracts to be used, especially in English law where the principle of precedent must encourage the adoption of standardised contracts. As industrial enterprise is a fairly recent phenomenon we would expect the type of contracts found in agriculture to have much influence on those in industry.

In societies in which land is owned three types of rental contract are found. The landlord may let the land either for a fixed monetary payment (a pure rental contract); or for a payment which is a certain share of the crop (a share-cropping contract); or he may hire workers, paying them a wage and specifying the job to be done (a pure wage contract). Share-cropping has been much studied (Bardhan and Srinivasan [1971], Cheung [1969] and Johnson [1950]) and provides the theoretical analysis for this discussion. The division of risk between the two parties in this market is clear. Because of uncertainty resulting from the level of output during the year and the price of agricultural goods in the market, the landlord will take all the risk in a pure wage contract, some of it in a share-cropping contract and none of it in a pure rental contract.

The degree of control of the landlord over the individual changes as the contract changes. The wage-earner would in general have little or no control over the job he does whilst the farmer who pays a monetary rent would have almost complete control. Share-cropping contracts are often associated with interference by the landlord in the running of the farm, for good reasons as will be seen later.

We see then that in these three differing markets the contract between the parties specified the amount of risk to be borne as well as the degree of participation of the individuals involved.[4]

Individuals are then faced with making decisions the outcomes of which are uncertain. They have to choose how much of this uncertainty they wish to bear and this will depend on their preferences over random variables, variables whose value is unknown but has a probability distribution associated with it.

3 PREFERENCES OVER RANDOM VARIABLES

Individuals then have some choice between relatively risky and relatively riskless positions in these markets. According to the amount of risk taken, one observes differing amounts of control for the individual. In order to analyse choices we need to know the structure of preferences in these markets. However, preferences are defined over variables which are now random, and not certain, so we are not able to proceed to a utility model immediately. Let us suppose that individuals know the probability distribution of the random variables they are concerned with. We are thus not making the distinction between risk and uncertainty[5] as to whether the probability distribution is known or not, and treat the words and risk and uncertainty synonymously. The mean and variance of the distribution is then known and one approach has been to limit preferences between random variables to choices amongst differing means and variances. The problem is that one cannot find a utility function, as a function of the random variables, which describes people's actions, as the realised values of the arguments would not be known when the choice is made. The solution that has been adopted for this problem is that of maximising expected utility. This would be the same as the representation of preferences by a utility function in the certain case, and also, it involves the whole of the distribution of the random variables rather than just the first and second moments, although these still have an important role. We use the expected utility maximisation hypothesis as a vehicle for determining individual's preferences amongst random variables. The assumptions required for this are described by Malinvaud [1972] and one should be aware of the restrictions on behaviour implied by these assumptions. The so-called strong independence axiom (see Malinvaud [1953]) in particular has strong restrictions on the structure of the indifference map.

We must ask whether we accept these assumptions for our purposes. Experiments have been conducted to check the validity of expected utility maximisation and the shape of the utility function, although they have been concerned with a particular type of uncertainty, preferences between gambles. Mostellor and Nogee [1951] found 'that the notion that people behave in such a way as to maximise their expected utility is not unreasonable', although Rosett [1971] concludes: 'The extent to which subjects' behaviour conforms to the expected utility hypothesis is powerfully affected by the complexity of the decision with which they are faced, and by the exact nature of the experiment.' For the markets in which we are interested it would be difficult, if not impossible, to verify experimentally the expected utility hypotheses. We must therefore rely on acceptance of the assumptions.

Unfortunately the strong independence assumption, that preference between a convex combination of x and z and the same convex combination of y and z should be independent of z, would not seem to be immediately acceptable. It is easy to imagine the form of contract entered into by an individual in all the three markets quoted depending on the amount and nature of the risk being taken in other aspects of an individual's life. However, there seems little alternative to adopting the expected utility hypothesis and perhaps one should do this as long as one is aware of the special properties of preferences implied.

Maximising expected utility gives the demand for uncertain goods. When one of the goods is certain, a trade-off between certainty and uncertainty can be found. This trade-off will just be an indifference curve. One can calculate whether an individual prefers certainty to uncertainty or vice versa and by how much. A measure of the amount is the risk premium which is the reduction in expected consumption which is traded off for elimination of uncertainty.

4 · CROP-SHARING TENANCIES AND RISK-SHARING

We now have the apparatus to discuss the models of Stiglitz [1974] and Newbery [1973]. These papers are primarily concerned with the third of our markets, that of agricultural production. Uncertainty is clearly a vital factor in determining the structure of the industry, the uncertainty of the level of output arising from the inputs applied meaning that the payments to factors will be somewhat uncertain. The paradigm of production is that there are two inputs, land and labour, giving a single homogeneous output. What payments will these inputs receive? This will depend on the form of wage contracts and who makes the production decisions. Newbery considers a farmer, paying both land and labour a fixed rate, who can hire any amount of labour and land so as to maximise his expected utility of income. This results in marginal products of factors being not necessarily equal to factor payments, but both differ by the same proportion so that the marginal rate of substitution still equals the ratio of factor payments.

In this case the farmer makes a profit above the payment of land and labour. (He may supply either the labour or the land himself so that by profit we mean income above that which he receives for inputs he supplies himself.) He also bears all the risk associated with production. What would be the consequences of the farmer sharing out the risk with the other participants in production? We take a new contract system where the rent of land is a share of the output, the share-cropping contract we have already mentioned. Traditional analysis (see Marshall

[1920], Gale Johnson [1950], Bardhan and Srinivasan [1971]) has concentrated on the possible loss of efficiency, and hence Pareto suboptimality, arising from this type of contract. If the farmer supplies his own labour then the amount of effort applied by him to the land will be that for which the marginal disutility of work equals the marginal reward for effort, which is his share of the marginal product.

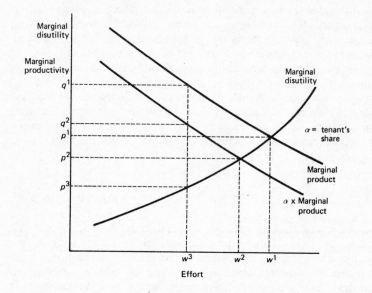

FIG. 9.1

For the situation in Figure 1, the crop-sharing contract leads to a lower amount of work being applied to the land than at the efficient point, where the amount of labour supplied is such that the marginal product of labour equals the marginal disutility of labour. The farmer also receives marginal reward p^2 which is lower than p^1. If the land is rented at a fixed rent and the farmer chooses the amount of labour he applies then he will provide amount w^1 and earn marginal payment p^1. In the latter case the farmer takes all the risk, but receives a higher marginal reward; whereas in the former case the risk is shared but the marginal reward lowered. A landlord hiring workers and paying them a fixed wage will be able to pay them a lower marginal rate, p^3 say, but will consequently obtain less effort, w^3. If the amount of effort required by the landlord were to be w^3 then the landlord could obtain this, given no restrictions on the supply of labour, at a marginal rate of pay of p^3 for a fixed rate system, q^2 for a share-cropping system and q^1 for a rental system. The higher the marginal payment though, the greater the amount of risk taken, and also, in actual fact, the amount of control over the job situation. We could observe the three systems in operation, though, if the appropriate risk premiums were equal to the wage differentials.

If we return to the analysis of share-cropping system, we see that for a fixed amount of land the share-cropper undersupplies effort for a Pareto optimum. If he rents as much land as he wishes then he will rent more and more land until the position where the marginal productivity of land worked by him is zero. In Figure 9.1 the marginal productivity curve moves outwards as the amount of land rented increases with the usual neo-classical assumption of the marginal product of one factor being an increasing function of the other factor. However, under the rental system the amount of land rented will be determined by where the marginal product of land equals the rental rate. Share-croppers may then use land inefficiently, attempting to obtain tenancy of as much land as possible and then applying small amounts of effort to it, so that the marginal product of labour is large.

In the wage system the risk is taken by the landlord whilst in the rental system the risk is taken by the worker, so that one might expect that the outcome of the share-cropping system would be that of a certain mixture of wage and rent payments. Newbery proves that if the effort supplied by the farmer is specified in a share-cropping contract then both parties are made no worse off by a mixture of fixed wage and fixed rent contracts. However, share-cropping is shown to be a useful contract when wages are also uncertain. The possibility of completely secure employment and real wages does seem rather unlikely, and in the markets considered in Section 2 the differences between contracts were differences between types of risk. Let us suppose that wages are uncertain but that the wage uncertainty is not necessarily correlated with output uncertainty. We take $Y = \theta F(L, T) E(\theta) = 1 \pi W =$ wage rate $E(\pi) = 1$ where Y is the output corresponding to L units of labour and T units of land. Newbery then shows share-cropping to be attractive, in that production would be inefficient; but a share-cropping system would be efficient if an equilibrium existed where tenants chose the most attractive contract available and landlords specified the available contracts by choosing the rental share and land-labour ratio to maximise the net return per acre to the landlord subject to the contract being taken up. The equilibrium return to the landlord must of course be equal in all contracts. The reason for inefficiency is that, for maximisation of the tenant's expected utility, the expectation of the tenant's marginal utility multiplied by marginal product of labour, $\dfrac{\partial E}{\partial L}$, will equal the expectation of marginal utility multiplied by the wage rate, πW. In general the lack of independence between the output uncertainty and wage rate uncertainty, θ and π, will cause the marginal product of labour to depend on the landlord's utility function. So that even if all landlords know the distributions of θ and π they will have differing marginal products of labour if their utility functions differ.

Under a share-cropping system where the amount of labour is specified, and there is equilibrium where landlord's returns per acre are equal and maximised, the labour-land ratio should be equal on all plots and so marginal products are equal and efficiency results. Stiglitz examines the contracts formed in the economy by individuals. Let us consider now the amount of labour supplied to be fixed.

For the simplest case, where all landlords and workers are identical, only one contract will be observed and it is possible to characterise this contract by properties of the utility functions of the individuals. The type of contract, not surprisingly, depends on risk averseness. If one of the groups is risk-neutral, that is when marginal utility is constant, so that variance has no effect on preferences, then that group absorbs all the risk and a pure wage or pure rent system will be observed. If both groups were risk-averse then a share-cropping system would occur in which the group more relatively risk-averse takes a smaller proportion of risk than it does of output. When individuals differ, different contracts will be observed and the labour – land ratio will vary between farms. Landlords more risk-averse than their workers will give their workers a greater share and so will have greater labour – land ratio. If the amount of labour supplied is variable the tenants now have to maximise their expected utility of income with respect to the amount of labour supplied as well as the type of contract signed (characterised by the share). If the cost of enforcing a contract is zero and the amount of work is observable then the amount of labour supplied by the worker will be specified and production will be efficient. In the pure rental case no such specification is made. However for a landlord hiring labour the specification of the job and effort will be greater. However there are usually costs of supervision and it may be cheaper for some form of incentive scheme to be provided. This scheme could be of a revenue-sharing 'bonus' system. Of course, this is nothing other than a share-cropping scheme. A 'piece-rate' scheme is a form of share-cropping for if the piece rate is W and the value of unit output is p then $\dfrac{W}{p}$ is the share of the worker. Share cropping may then be observed even with risk-neutral landlords if supervision is necessary. The extent of the bonus scheme will depend on the extent to which careful control is necessary and this depends on the elasticity of substitution in production. Stiglitz finds that if the elasticity of substitution of effort per worker for workers per acre is greater than one, then the worker receives a mean income greater than the mean marginal product, and vice versa.

We can see that the landlord, less risk-averse than his tenants, in this system is trying to reduce the control of the tenant over output. If supervision is possible and cheap the landlord will as fully specify the job as possible. When the amount of effort supplied cannot be controlled, or control is expensive, the landlord will want to provide incentives and share-cropping or a wage-rent system will be used. This latter system could be a landlord hiring workers and requiring them to have shares in the farm.

5 DEVELOPMENT OF CONTRACTS

We mentioned earlier that new contracts formed often reflect the type of contracts in existence. The development of land contracts may well be of interest. Marshall pointed out the general vagueness of contracts. This vagueness seems to have increased over time as provisions in land contracts, which were of a barter nature, were forgotten. Thus in Russia the abolition of serfdom in 1861 caused unrest because of the peasants' traditional view of the social contract implied. Nove [1969] has described the peasants' view of the role of themselves and their landlords thus:

Serfdom had been imposed largely for state reasons, to provide an economic basis for the service gentry to enable them to serve the Tsar with land, and peasants had an obligation to maintain the gentry in the service of the Tsar. When in 1762 this duty of service was finally abandoned, this removed the only possible justification for the peasants' attachment to the land, as the peasants understood it. Let me illustrate the original *raison d'être* of serfdom with a historical example. In 1571 a Tartar invasion from the Crimea caused many thousands of peasants and their families to be led away into slavery. To prevent a recurrence of these events a standing army was necessary, and a strong monarchy. Many peasants understood this. They were in a position to evade their obligations by moving eastwards and southwards across an open frontier, and in fact did so on a large scale during the wars of Ivan the Terrible, which reduced revenue, numbers or recruits and the value of land grants to the gentry. The peasants' attachment to the soil thus had a rational purpose. However, by the late eighteenth century the gentry had the right to become merely parasitic landlords (though in fact many of them did continue to serve the state in various capacities), while the majority of the peasants were reduced to a state of slavery. The belief survived among them that 'they were the lord's but the land was God's'.

The so called 'mercantilisation' of agriculture has been described by Hicks [1969]. It is a familiar theme, the existence of privileges and duties in primitive economies. There are good reasons for these to exist, the existence of externalities, lack of markets in general, the need to share unavoidable risks and increases in productivity through division of labour. Hicks points out that the exchange of the labour of the peasant for the military and administrative duties of the lords of the manor was no different from exchange in more modern markets, except that the medium of money was not used. It is sometimes forgotten how recent the general use of money is. Division of labour would make it efficient to have a class of peasants and a class of lords. The exchange takes place by means of payments in kind both of produce and labour. Whitelock [1952] in a survey of Anglo-Saxon England has outlined the duties of the peasant:

> We learn also what could be demanded from the *gebur*, a peasant who had been given his holding – a quarter of a hide – by the lord, and supplied with two oxen, one cow, and six sheep as initial stock, seven acres already sown, tools for his work and utensils for his house. In return, after the lapse of a year, he is to give two days' work every week, and three days at harvest time, and from Candlemas to Easter, unless he should be using his horses on the lord's service. He is to pay a rent of tenpence at Michaelmas, twenty-three sesters of barley and two hens at Martinmas, a young sheep, to twopence, at Easter. In rotation with others of his kind, he is to keep watch at his lord's fold in the period between Martinmas and Easter. In addition, he must plough one acre a week in the autumn ploughing, fetch the seed from the lord's barn, and plough three acres extra as 'boonwork', two acres in return for pasture rights. As part of his rent, he ploughs a further three acres and sows them with his own seed. He joins with one of his fellows in keeping a staghound for his lord, and he gives six loaves to the latter's swineherd when he drives his herd of swine to the mast pasture. On his death, his lord inherits his goods.

However in an economy in which there is an excess supply of land, so that the price of land is zero, the peasant may be induced to escape his part of the contract by moving to new land. Perhaps for these reasons the feudal system, in which workers were tied to the land, was introduced. This rise of markets in towns forced changes in this system. One change was the use of the medium of money, another the 'inveterate Teutonic tendency to treat public office as private property and therefore as something that could be transmitted by inheritance' (Morier [1876]). So that by the end of the nineteenth century even landowners believed they had no direct role as landowners. For example Thompson [1963] quotes the following reply of the Duke of Northumberland: 'In answer to the question: "As a coal owner what service do you perform to the community?", the Duke could only say, "As owner of the coal I do not think I perform any service to the community – not as owner of the coal!"' (*Report of the Royal Commission on the Coal Industry*, 1919). (Although it perhaps should be added that a modern economist might think the duke short-sighted as the determination of the rate of extraction and exploration of the coal would be an important decision taken only by the duke. At that time the rate of extraction would have been determined by private coalowners only and the goal of guaranteeing future private income in response to fluctuations in coal prices would be necessary if an optimal extraction rate was to be set. Thus the duke may well have been unaware of the duties he was performing.)

Returning to the former cause of change, inconvenience of handling payments in kind and uncertainties about the prices of this produce in markets seem to have made landlords prefer monetary rents. Thus the town of New Alresford in Hampshire was built ' . . . simply to reap advantages from a place where building lots were let against money rents instead of rents in land. It made procedure simpler and income safer.'[6] Thus a transition from a crop-sharing system to a rental system was made. The rental system had provisions for the security of tenure of the farmer, for otherwise agricultural improvements might not have been made, as well as the ability of the landlord to evict the tenant, for otherwise there would be no sanction against non-payment of rent, see Marshall [1920] for example. This system is that of tenant farming. An alternative system was the wage contract system which grew up in towns, and in due course it became the model for the contract between employer and employee in early industrial production. This system, the putting-out system, involved the entrepreneur paying the worker a piece-rate wage for the work he did. The employee worked at home on articles, pieces of cloth for example, given to him by the entrepreneur. The origin and development of this system have been described by Pollard [1965]. The system did not last long. The workers had complete control over the amount of work they did, and the methods of production used; however, they took no risks, being paid a fixed rate for the number of finished articles they produced. Pollard describes how the system ' . . . had to depend on the work performed in innumerable tiny domestic workshop units, unsupervised and unsupervisable. Such incompatibility was bound to set up tension and to drive the merchants to seek new ways of production, imposing their own managerial achievements and practices on the productive sector.'

The factors involved were the uncertainty of supply of effort, the quality of output and prevention of theft, although coincidentally technical changes were making the domestic system inefficient. However, a form of the share-cropping system, that of sub-contracting, was fairly important in large-scale production. It was used heavily for example in the building of canals and railways. As well as being a way of increasing the technical knowledge at a builder's disposal, by bringing in specialist contractors, it also spread the risks, these being considerable.

However, the tenant farming system was not completely dominant in the United Kingdom. An experiment with agricultural participation was made by Lord Wantage on his estate at Ardington in Berkshire. This estate and its operation has been described by Havinden [1966]. During the time of the agricultural depression in the late nineteenth century the number of tenants fell dramatically, from ten in 1868 to one in 1891. The farms vacated were added to the home farm run by Lord Wantage. On his enlarged estate a profit-sharing scheme was initiated. Lord Wantage's philosophy was that '[The labourer] is not merely a human machine, paid for so many hours' work, whether it is done conscientiously and intelligently, or negligently and indifferently, but that he has a practical and tangible interest in the successful working of the farm.' Profit-sharing also would act as an incentive scheme, supervision being difficult on a farm of 13,000 acres. The profit was calculated as the difference between all payments and receipts, allowing rent at £1 an acre and 5 per cent interest on capital. However, because of variation in profits a bonus was paid on a six-yearly average of profits. A bonus was paid on a quarter of profits, this bonus being non-negative, so that the labourer did not take any share in possible losses. The bonus was distributed according to a share system, the number of shares depending on the status of the worker. In 1887 the bonus was £3 (the weekly wage was 10s) but because of declining agricultural fortunes this fell continually to 10s, in 1893 being paid out of reserves. The declining bonus led to feelings of disappointment and frustration; the labourers feeling that they were losing through no fault of their own, the decline being due to weather and food prices. These feelings led to the abandonment of the system and the introduction of piece rates.

We have seen that the crop-sharing contract is a useful one for sharing the risk involved when neither of the parties is willing to take it on. It is also useful as an incentive method and when other contracts involve uncertainty. However, the landlord will wish to enforce a minimum labour – land ratio in order to ensure that the marginal productivity of land is kept at a certain level. These results are derived on the basis of all individuals in the groups being identical. If this is not so then some individuals may wish to provide more effort than the minimum. Others may have preferred to apply less effort but are prohibited from doing so. Thus the contracts involve varying amounts of flexibility. The wage contract involves detailed job specification and hours; the share contract involves minimum effort, and perhaps minimum capital and all other inputs; the rental contract has most flexibility for the farmer, for as long as he pays the rent the organisation of work is completely up to himself. We have not considered explicit utility from participation. This will depend on how participation is measured. If the share of output is a suitable proxy for the amount of participation then the necessary conditions for a maximum of expected utility for the tenant will include a constant term and will have the same effect as a reduction in the share of output. However, in an industrial context, the wage contract may also be uncertain and we have seen that the share contract provides an efficient equilibrium. But perhaps we should regard individuals as obtaining utility from other contexts than income, and this will lead us to an expected utility analysis involving more than one uncertain variable.

Perhaps the most important point is that share contracts can be replaced by mixed wage/rent contracts, and thus the risk of the enterprise can be shared by this means, providing that share-holding workers will have a certain amount of control over the firm's decisions. The price for having control over decisions appears to be the risk taken. The price in terms of risk may always be sufficiently high to dominate the utility obtained from participation in decision-making. This may explain the often surprisingly low-voiced demands for participation in decision-making, although the lack of control of shareholders may provide some reason for this. If it is possible for a shareholder to have a degree of control over the firm then the worker can obtain a suitable degree of participation by the granting of an appropriate number of shares. The problem then becomes one of social choice. How can the interests of many different people with conflicting interests be reconciled? The traditional method is the annual election of directors, which reflects the parliamentary base of Western society but may not be appropriate, as directors are not mandated nor do they considered detailed proposals.

6 CONCLUSIONS

Although this is not a piece of original work, I hope that pulling together the thoughts of others on widely differing fields gives perspectives not realised before. Markets appear to equate the degree of participation to the amount of risk taken. This is no more than the theory of Knight, that the profit made by an entrepreneur is the payment for taking risk, would suggest. If participation, then, is just the sharing of entrepreneurship between workers and managers, the workers will have to take the appropriate amount of risk. However, this risk has a price. If we accept that decisions are made by maximising the expected value of utility function, and we see that it is not obvious that this should be so, then there is a certain combination of goods indifferent to the uncertain combination. So in a competitive world the more participation one has, the lower the indifferent combination of certain goods will be. It may well be that the gain in utility from *any* amount of participation will not offset the loss in utility from the resulting amount of risk borne. Whether this is so is now for analysis by empirical uncertainty models.

NOTES

1. I am grateful to J. Aldrich, E. R. Chang and D. F. Heathfield for valuable advice and encouragement.
2. We leave the concept of increasing risk undefined. A discussion of the problems of distinguishing increasing risk may be found in Peleg [1975] and Rothschild and Stiglitz [1970].
3 As housing rents are often cost-determined and mortgage repayments are interest rate-determined it is possible for rises in housing rents to coincide with a fall in existing mortgage repayments, as at present (March 1976).
4. We may note that precisely the same is found in the distinction between debentures (non-voting, but with a prior claim on assets) and ordinary shares.
5. See Knight [1921].
6. See Pevsner [1967].

REFERENCES

Bardhan, P. K., and Srinivasan T. N. [1971], 'Cropsharing Tenancy in Agriculture' *American Economic Review*, 61.

Cheung, S. N. S. [1969], *The Theory of Share Tenancy* (Chicago: University of Chicago Press).

Havinden M. A. [1966], *Estate Villages* (Lund, Humphries).

Hicks J. R. [1969], *A Theory of Economic History* (Clarendon Press).

Johnson D. Gale [1950], 'Resource Allocation under share contracts', *Journal of Political Economy*, 58.

Knight, F. H. [1921], *Risk, Uncertainty and Profit* (Boston: Houghton Mifflin).

Malinvaud, E. [1972], *Lectures on Micro Economic Theory* (Amsterdam: North-Holland).

Malinvaud, E., [1953], 'A note on von Neumann-Morgenstern's Strong Independence Axiom', *Econometrica*, 21.

Marshall, A. [1920], *Principles of Economics* (Macmillan).

Morier, R. B. D. [1876], 'The Agrarian Legislation of Prussia during the present century', in Probyn [1876].

Mosteller, F., and Nogee P. [1951], 'An experimental measurement of utility', *Journal of Political Economy*, 59.

Newbery, D. M. G. [1973], 'Cropsharing Tenancy in an Equilibrium Model' (mimeo), *paper given to Econometric Society*, Oslo, August.

Nove, A., [1967], *An Economic History of the U.S.S.R.* (Penguin).

Peleg, B. [1975], 'Efficient Random Variables', *Journal of Mathmatical Economies*.

Pevsner, N., [1967], *The Buildings of England: Hampshire and the Isle of Wight*. (Penguin).

Pollard, S., [1965], *The Genesis of Modern Management* (Edward Arnold).

Probyn, J. W., [1876], *Systems of Land Tenure in Various Countries* (Cassell).

Rosett, R. N., [1971], 'Weak Experimental Verification of the Expected Utility Hypothesis', *Review of Economic Studies*, 38.

Rothschild, M., and Stiglitz, J. E. [1970], Increasing Risk I: a definition', *Journal of Economic Theory*, 2.

Stiglitz, J. E., [1974], 'Incentives and Risk Sharing in Sharecropping', *Review of Economic Studies*, 41.

Shannon, H. A., [1931], 'The Coming of General Limited Liability', *Economic History*, II.

Thompson, F. M. L. [1963], *English Landed Society in the Nineteenth century* (Routledge & Kegan Paul).

Whitelock, D., [1952], *The Beginnings of English Society* (Penguin).

Name Index

Subject Index